D0130487

'This programme has answered a lot of the questions I had about the pupils I am working with and has enabled me to support them in a more effective and informed way. The resources are clearly linked to the curriculum, making it easy to include them in planning. I will be recommending this book to all the schools I support.'

Nicki Jennings, SEMH and Behaviour Specialist, Giraffe Training

'Beyond relevant in Education right now! With increasing access to social media, children from a young age require high quality education on positive body image and self worth. This book prov' a practical way to do just that for educators, including key links to the national curriculum and the PSHE Association.'

Abbigael Bainton, teacher and PSHE co-ordinator

I2781546

by the same author

Building Happiness, Resilience and Motivation in Adolescents
A Positive Psychology Curriculum for Well-Being
Ruth MacConville and Tina Rae
ISBN 978 1 84905 261 0
eISBN 978 0 85700 548 9

of related interest

Your Body is Brilliant
Body Respect for Children
Sigrun Danielsdottir
Illustrated by Bjork Bjarkdottir
ISBN 978 1 84819 221 8
eISBN 978 0 85701 179 4

Healthy Mindsets for Super Kids
A Resilience Programme for Children Aged 7–14
Stephanie Azri
ISBN 978 1 84905 315 0
eISBN 978 0 85700 698 1

Helping Children to Build Self-Esteem
A Photocopiable Activities Book
2nd Edition
Deborah M. Plummer
ISBN 978 1 84310 488 9
eISBN 978 1 84642 609 4

Believing You Can is the First Step to Achieving
A CBT and Attribution Retraining Programme to Improve Self-Belief in Students aged 8–12
Alicia R Chodkiewicz and Christopher Boyle
ISBN 978 1 84905 625 0
eISBN 978 1 78450 098 6

Starving the Anxiety Gremlin for Children Aged 5–9
A Cognitive Behavioural Therapy Workbook on Anxiety Management
Kate Collins-Donnelly
ISBN 978 1 84905 492 8
eISBN 978 0 85700 902 9

Starving the Anger Gremlin for Children Aged 5–9
A Cognitive Behavioural Therapy Workbook on Anger Management
Kate Collins-Donnelly
ISBN 978 1 84905 493 5
eISBN 978 0 85700 885 5

POSITIVE BODY IMAGE
FOR KIDS

A Strengths-Based Curriculum for Children Aged 7–11

RUTH MACCONVILLE

Jessica Kingsley *Publishers*
London and Philadelphia

First published in 2017
by Jessica Kingsley Publishers
73 Collier Street
London N1 9BE, UK
and
400 Market Street, Suite 400
Philadelphia, PA 19106, USA

www.jkp.com

Copyright © Ruth MacConville 2017

Front cover image source: Shutterstock®. The cover image is for illustrative
purposes only, and any person featuring is a model.

All rights reserved. No part of this publication may be reproduced in any material form (including
photocopying, storing in any medium by electronic means or transmitting) without the written permission
of the copyright owner except in accordance with the provisions of the law or under terms of a licence
issued in the UK by the Copyright Licensing Agency Ltd. www.cla.co.uk or in overseas territories by the
relevant reproduction rights organisation, for details see www.ifrro.org. Applications for the copyright
owner's written permission to reproduce any part of this publication should be addressed to the publisher.

All pages marked ⤓ can be downloaded at www.jkp.com/voucher using the code
MACCONVILLEPOSITIVE for personal use with this program, but may not be
reproduced for any other purposes without the permission of the publisher.

All pages marked ✓ may be photocopied for personal use with this program, but may not
be reproduced for any other purposes without the permission of the publisher.

Warning: The doing of an unauthorised act in relation to a copyright work may
result in both a civil claim for damages and criminal prosecution.

Library of Congress Cataloging in Publication Data
Names: MacConville, Ruth, author.
Title: Positive body image for kids : a strengths-based curriculum for
    children aged 7-11 / Ruth MacConville.
Description: London ; Philadelphia : Jessica Kingsley Publishers, 2017. |
    Includes bibliographical references.
Identifiers: LCCN 2016029959 | ISBN 9781849055390 (alk. paper)
Subjects: LCSH: Body image in children. | Body image in children--Study and
    teaching (Elementary)
Classification: LCC BF723.B6 M33 2017 | DDC 618.92/8526--dc23

British Library Cataloguing in Publication Data
A CIP catalogue record for this book is available from the British Library

ISBN 978 1 84905 539 0
eISBN 978 1 78450 047 4

Printed and bound in Great Britain

CONTENTS

Introduction 7

1. Why Do We Need to Teach Children About Body Image? 11

2. The Purpose of this Resource and Links to the Curriculum 23

3. General Guidance on Delivering the Programme 35

4. Staff Training 65

5. The Sessions 81

6. Involving Parents and Carers 225

Further information 238

References 246

Index 250

For Andrew, Matthew and Yvonne, with love.

INTRODUCTION

Thin is in. This is the message that the media delivers daily. Our children receive a glut of information – from magazines, advertisers, songs, films and TV – that purports to tell them about the ultra-thin ideal. And the grip that the media has on their attention is tighter and starts earlier than ever before. There is no doubt that the self-image, ambitions and values of numerous children have been damaged by the commercial frenzy that hammers into them that what matters most is how they look. Part of this frenzy is thanks to the impact of the media, with its unrealistic imagery, airbrushing and size zero models. The media has created an image-obsessed world where messages about the right looks are delivered to children every day without discrimination, and there is ample evidence that the more mainstream media girls consume, the more importance they place on being sexy and pretty.

The escalating estimates of appearance-related distress in children make for scary reading. In 1999, Grogan wrote that body dissatisfaction has a high prevalence in the population from the age of eight years upwards, and now, almost two decades later, that figure has significantly increased and children are also affected at an increasingly early age. A study by University of Florida professor Stacey Tantleff-Dunn and Sharon Hayes, published in the *British Journal of Developmental Psychology* in 2010, showed that half of three- to five-year-old girls worry about being fat, and that by age nine, half of them have already been on a diet. Such psychological vulnerability can lead to feelings of low self-esteem and body dissatisfaction. Psychoanalyst and author Susie Orbach (2010) observes in her book *Bodies* that 'without a body that girls (and boys) feel all right about nothing much else in their lives feels okay'. Body dissatisfaction can diminish children's self-esteem and demand their attention at a time when it should be available for important developmental tasks. It is well documented that, once established, body dissatisfaction is difficult to reverse.

In this book I draw on my practical experience in schools as well as on recent research to provide an approach that will enable schools and parents to intervene before unhealthy attitudes have a chance to take hold. Providing children with practical interventions at an early age that are designed to reinforce the basic building blocks of healthy living and celebrate their strengths, talents and innate body esteem is our greatest hope of preventing the development of body dissatisfaction.

Children need to hear clear messages that enable them to navigate successfully through the plethora of high-powered advertising and media messages that convey to them that what matters most is how they look.

The curriculum that forms the backbone of this book has been designed as a structured, practical resource to take primary-aged children aged between five and eleven years of age on a journey of self-reflection, where they become more in control of their lives. To be most effective, it is critical that the programme is recognised as part of the school or setting's overall approach to personal, social, health and economic education (PSHE) and as a part of their statutory safeguarding duties in line with the guidance documents *Working Together to Safeguard Children* (Department for Education 2015) and *Keeping Children Safe in Education* (Department for Education 2015). These vital links, which are imperative to the success of the programme, are described in more detail in the upcoming chapters of this book.

The Positive Body Image programme can be used in a range of settings, including mainstream schools, where it can be used with whole classes or small groups, and specialist settings such as schools or resource centres for children with a range of special educational needs and disabilities, such as those with social, emotional and mental health (SEMH), physical or sensory impairments. Although body image has traditionally been viewed as the domain of schools, the programme can also be used successfully in youth clubs and in similar enterprises for children and young people where there are opportunities to give children the encouragement to support each other to feel good about themselves, develop their strengths and talents, and resist media pressures about the way that they should look. In the 2014 Girlguiding UK survey, children reported that constructive and positive emotional support from their peers had a significant effect on their ability to cope with media pressures about their appearance.

The programme aims to enable children to build the resilience to withstand media pressures, recognise their strengths and talents, and feel positive about their appearance. It has been designed to introduce children to the practical skills of healthy living through the use of fun, educational activities. The sessions are therefore interactive and largely based on partner and group discussion to ensure that the children learn more about themselves and others. In the spirit of positive psychology – one of the fields of study on which the programme is based – the sessions are intended to be delivered with a sense of fun and celebration to ensure that *all* children are engaged and inspired. Although the themes and sessions have been designed to build on and reinforce each other, it is possible to select and use single sessions and activities if that is more appropriate to any given situation. Children are encouraged to practise the skills and ideas that are introduced in the sessions in their everyday lives so that they are able to initiate positive changes for themselves. Further advice and guidance on delivering the programme can be found in Chapter three of this resource.

This book is written in six parts. Chapter one describes the purpose of the resource and how it contributes to a school's statutory duties. These include the National Curriculum, the safeguarding agenda, and the spiritual, moral, social and cultural (SMSC) programme of study. As part of section 5 inspections in England, when making a judgement about a school, Ofsted must consider how all schools show how well their pupils are developing in SMSC education. Chapter two also shows how the programme links to the PSHE Education Programme of Study (2014). Chapter three provides general guidance on delivering the programme. This guidance includes a brief introduction to the areas of research on which the programme is based, suggestions on how to get the whole school involved, advice on scheduling the programme, the structure of the sessions, and the resources that are required to deliver the programme. It also includes practical advice on safeguarding, how to handle, and create a safe and positive learning environment, and supporting different learning needs. Chapter four contains training materials that can be used to introduce to staff the Positive Body Image programme. It includes a presentation with slides, facilitator notes and practical activities. This is recommended reading for all members of staff and especially for those who will be delivering the programme. Chapter five consists of the 16 sessions that form the programme. The final chapter provides guidance and practical approaches to involving parents and carers in the programme, including suggestions on how to deliver a workshop for them. The book ends with a list of further information giving websites and recommended reading for children, parents and carers, and schools.

All pages marked ↓ can be downloaded at www.jkp.com/voucher using the code MACCONVILLEPOSITIVE.

CHAPTER 1

WHY DO WE NEED TO TEACH CHILDREN ABOUT BODY IMAGE?

The concept of body image is not new. Paul Ferdinand Schilder (1886–1940), an Austrian psychiatrist and psychoanalyst, and student of Sigmund Freud, was the first to coin the phrase in his book *The Image and Appearance of the Human Body*, published in 1935. In this publication, Schilder argued, ahead of his time, that body image is affected by our interactions and the attitudes of others.

Body image is a broad concept that refers to the way people think and feel about their appearance. It includes ideas about how our body looks: size and shape, skin colour, facial features and our clothing. For people with disabilities, body image also encompasses feelings about 'visible differences' and their use of aids and equipment, for example hearing aids, wheelchairs and prostheses. The mental picture of how individuals feel about their appearance and how attractive they perceive themselves to be to others is independent of their actual appearance. Anyone, whatever they look like, can have a positive or a negative body image. There are a range of factors that contribute to a person's body image; responses from parents, other family members, teachers, other important adults, peers and the media all play a significant role in influencing how an individual feels about their appearance. Our body image is not static. It changes in response to feedback from others.

A key task of childhood and adolescence is to develop one's self-concept and sense of identity. World-renowned body image expert Thomas Cash (2008) explains that a positive body image plays a vital role in fostering healthy psychological development and is the largest contributor to self-esteem and self-concept in children. Dr Byrony Bamford (2015), consultant clinical psychologist at The London Centre for Eating Disorders and Body Image, told her audience at a recent Public Policy Exchange Symposium Event entitled *Mental Health and Young People: Promoting a Positive and Healthy Body Image*:

> Learning about your own appearance is central to the world of a child. Distress associated with appearance can therefore be utterly debilitating and can easily be carried forward into adulthood. We should care about body image disorder because it increases rates of disordered eating in young people…even in the absence of an eating disorder, body image concerns can be impairing, preoccupying and distressing, taking up a great deal of mental energy and detracting from their quality of life.

It is important to make the distinction here between body image and self-esteem. Body image encompasses what we think of our appearance, while self-esteem includes our feelings about our own worth as individuals. Self-esteem and body image are inextricably linked and together form the fabric of how we feel about ourselves. Individuals with healthy self-esteem usually feel positive about their appearance, while those with low self-esteem are frequently dissatisfied with how they look. Equally, feeling good about one's appearance enhances self-esteem, whereas feelings of discontentment can undermine it.

WHAT IS A POSITIVE BODY IMAGE?

A positive body image gives us the freedom and flexibility to be ourselves; it is about having a balanced view and knowing that our appearance is only one part of who we are. The effects of a positive body image are far-reaching; feeling good about one's appearance instils an optimistic attitude that attracts friends, builds confidence and enables an individual to be successful in a variety of domains. According to the young people interviewed by Kate Collins-Donnelly (2014), a positive body image means:

- being happy with how your body actually is

- feeling comfortable with your body

- feeling satisfied with how you look

- being confident in how you look

- realising that the 'perfect' body does not exist

- recognising that who you are as a person is more important than how you look

- not letting appearance rule your life

- believing the health of your body is more important than how it looks.

In her book *Real Kids Come in All Sizes*, psychotherapist Kathy Kater (2004) explains that the essence of a positive body image is to be in touch with and have confidence in our own experiences and positively regard our thoughts and feelings without doubt or judgement. Thoughts *about* this reality may be important to consider but they are secondary; what is most important is a secure sense of knowing our own individual inner experience. Healthy body esteem means maintaining our own integrity: we know what we need, even when those around us are not in agreement and may not support us. It also means not sacrificing the confident *knowing* of our own experience even as we tune into others'. Whether we are hungry or full, energetic or tired, or bored or interested, we know for certain that this feeling is true for us even if no one else feels the same and even if we know what we need isn't obtainable. Kater (2004, p.12) writes that 'the most notable aspect of positive body esteem is that, whether or not the outside world agrees, we are the ultimate authority on ourselves. We are *in* our body.'

THE KEY CHARACTERISTICS OF POSITIVE BODY IMAGE

Body appreciation

- Appreciating the health of the body.
- Appreciating the body for what it can do more than for its appearance.

Body acceptance and love

- Expressing comfort with and love for the body, despite not being completely satisfied with all its aspects.
- Choosing to focus on body assets rather than perceived body flaws.
- Avoiding potentially hazardous ways to alter appearance (for example, strict dieting, over-exercising, cosmetic surgery).

Optimism and a positive outlook

- Feeling that our inner qualities 'shine through' and boost our appearance and behaviour.
- Feeling good about ourselves, being optimistic and happy, which shows up as helping others, smiling, asserting ourselves, holding our head up high, standing tall and conveying confidence and well-being.

Broad conception of beauty

- Viewing a wide range of weights, shapes and appearances as beautiful.
- Believing that what makes people beautiful is carrying the self well, for example being groomed and confident rather than conforming to a media ideal.

Media literate

- Being aware that many media messages are unrealistic.
- Rejecting/challenging media images, for example pictures of ultra-thin models, and negative comments about our appearance that could undermine and damage our body image on a regular basis.

Unconditional acceptance from others

- Recognising body acceptance from others (for example, family, friends).
- Feeling loved, special and valued for who we are and our character strengths rather than for our appearance (when our appearance is mentioned by others, comments are usually complimentary and related to aspects within our control, such as clothes, grooming and hairstyle).

Finding others with a positive body image

- Choosing friends who also have a positive body image.

Listening to and taking care of the body

- Taking part in enjoyable activities and exercise.
- Having regular check-ups and seeking advice when unwell.
- Looking after the body, for example having healthy habits.
- Trusting the body to know when and how much to eat; eating a variety of foods that are enjoyable, healthy and keep the body performing well.
- Maintaining a stable weight based on our body type that is within the normal range.

(Adapted from Tylka 2011)

UNDERSTANDING BODY DISSATISFACTION

Dissatisfaction with one's body or a negative body image occurs when a person has negative thoughts and feelings about their body. It usually involves a difference between how people think they should look (their ideal body) and how they actually look (Dohnt and Tiggemann 2005; Grogan 2006; Wertheim and Paxton 2009). This can range from a mild preference for different body characteristics to severe distress associated with extreme behaviours to change the body or avoid criticism and/or disapproval. Body image dissatisfaction doesn't only refer to body shape and size – it may also include skin colour, fitness, facial characteristics, disabilities and ethnic diversity. In her book *Banish Your Body Image Thief,* Kate Collins-Donnelly (2014, pp.118–119) explains that because body dissatisfaction has become so widespread 'to many people the idea of having a positive body image is scary. This is because having a negative body image is all they know, whereas a positive body image is the unknown.'

Children who have a negative body image may:

- constantly worry about how they look

- be anxious about their weight

- have an unrealistic view of what they look like

- be preoccupied with parts of their body that they would like to be different

- compare themselves to others and wish that they looked like them

- feel insecure and blame it on their appearance

- believe that their life would be perfect if they could only change the way that they look.

The effect that body dissatisfaction can have on children and young people is significant. Body dissatisfaction consumes a great deal of energy and attention that children need for important developmental tasks, and as such it can interfere with the development of a child's sense of identity. Children who worry about their appearance constantly feel anxious and preoccupied, making it difficult for them to make friends, get along with others, accept compliments, recognise their strengths, or describe themselves in positive terms. Body dissatisfaction can also trigger feelings of shame and embarrassment in young people, making it difficult or even impossible for children to concentrate on school work, join in sports activities, or focus on other important life skills. Body dissatisfaction can also lead to depression and unhealthy weight control behaviours such as dieting, excessive exercising and, in extreme cases, the development of an eating disorder. In her book *I'm, Like, So Fat! Helping Your Teen Make Healthy Choices About Eating and Exercise in a Weight-Obsessed World,* researcher and professor at the School of Public Health at the University of Minnesota,

Dianne Neumark-Sztainer (2005, p.14), emphasises that 'if we take these links seriously, it's clear that, despite its increasing prevalence, body dissatisfaction should *not* be viewed as "normative discontent", i.e. an acceptable component of childhood development. Body dissatisfaction matters; it is not an inevitable part of being a child or young person'.

Individuals with an unhealthy body image tend to fall into four main groups:

1. Those who are moderately/severely dissatisfied with their appearance.

2. Those suffering body image disturbance as a result of an injury, wound, disfigurement or disability.

3. Those suffering from eating disorders.

4. Those suffering from extreme body image dissatisfaction that is indicative of *body dysmorphic disorder*.

BODY DYSMORPHIC DISORDER

For some people, up to 2 per cent of the population, an obsessive preoccupation with their appearance is the severe problem known as body dysmorphic disorder (BDD), a recently registered condition which was only reported on by the National Institute for Health and Care Excellence in 2005, and which is thought to be a form of obsessive compulsive disorder. As yet under-recognised and under-researched, it is defined as 'a preoccupation with some imagined defect in appearance'. Preliminary estimates suggest that it may be present in up to 8 per cent of cases of depression. It involves distress over any of the following:

• an imagined defect or physical anomaly

• body weight and shape concerns

• concerns with facial features, complexion and/or hair.

In her book *The Broken Mirror: Understanding and Treating Body Dysmorphic Disorder*, Katherine Phillips (2005) calls this condition 'the disorder of imagined ugliness' and explains that individuals with BDD have a grossly distorted view of what they look like, although to others they either look fine or have a barely noticeable defect. Phillips notes that although the majority of cases of BDD occur in adults, more than 70 per cent of their case histories indicate that their symptoms started in childhood. BDD affects girls and boys equally.

LAURA

In her book *The Story of Childhood: Growing Up in Modern Britain*, Libby Brooks (2006, p.201) describes the experiences of Laura, who has recently been diagnosed with BDD. Laura is a school refuser following bouts of playground bullying, and says her teachers didn't really notice what was going on until she had left the school, and by then it was far too late:

> When so many people start not to like you, you have to think it's something about you. I always feel like people judge me when they meet me and I think it must be something to do with the way I look. I maybe don't look good enough or look right enough for people to like me… When they started beating me up I actually remember thinking to myself, 'I want to look pretty.' Part of me thought something must look wrong with me for them to hate me so much and part of me thought if I become really pretty next time I see them that'll show them that I don't care what they did to me.

As is the case for so many individuals, Laura's BDD and her depression are inextricably linked, and as Thomas Cash (2008, p.3) explains:

> Self-disparagement and thoughts of hopelessness and helplessness about what you look like are depressing. In turn, this despondency, like quicksand, can further trap you in self-criticisms of your body. It becomes a vicious cycle of despair.

Laura gets so frustrated with the way she looks that she 'wears her make-up like armour, as though it will protect her from all onslaughts', but the more she tries to make herself look pretty the uglier she feels:

> I used to spend hours just staring in the mirror and it got quite bad, every morning, every evening. If I wanted to get to school on time I'd wake up at six in the morning, though I didn't have to leave till half-eight and sometimes I wouldn't get in till eleven… I think it's unfair that some people are born into life looking so much better than other people and they get treated better throughout their lives because of it… And I feel like people are always going to judge me because I don't look as good. (Brooks 2006, p.201)

> The trouble is, the longer Laura stays at home because she feels ugly, the more time she has to pour over those magazine images of supermodels and the less chance she has to compare herself with other girls with doughy skin and thick thighs. (Brooks 2006, p.207)

WHAT CAN CAUSE BODY DISSATISFACTION?

Studies that address the development of body image agree that body image is learned and is influenced by many factors that interact with each other. There is no single cause of body dissatisfaction. Rather, it is caused by a combination of the following factors:

- our cultural group and the society in which we live
- an individual's psychological make-up
- family relationships and the extent to which parents themselves buy into media pressures
- media influences.

The fact that all of these risk factors are so intertwined can make changes challenging.

Although exposure to the thin-as-ideal body borders on being ubiquitous in our society, Thomas Cash (2008, p.41) reminds us that 'cultures are not uniform'. For example, within the United States, the appreciation of fuller-figure bodies and the valuing of personal style and dress protect African-American children from developing body dissatisfaction. Associate professor in the Department of Nutrition, Food Studies and Public Health at New York University, Sharron Dalton (2004, p.182), recalls watching a jump rope contest involving African-American 'kids' from Harlem:

> These kids were big, but very active. The parents were cheering the contestants: 'Way to go big girl! Go, girl!' The winner of the final Dutch Double round – a heavy girl – would not likely to be chosen for the cheerleading squad in a high school just a few miles away, but here she was definitely the star of the day. These kids were supported by community activities and by affirmation for their participation, regardless of body size. This kind of parental and community support for active play will help them grow into their large size and help counter the forces that make them fat.

Dalton (2004, p.182) contrasts this scene with what would happen if there was a sound track with voices heckling these girls 'because their fat jiggles when they jump rope'. No need to guess what happens next: the big girl retreats indoors, takes comfort in snacking in front of the TV and concludes that jumping rope is only for skinny kids.

Although as Thomas Cash (2008) points out we may be tempted to dismiss other cultures' approaches to body image as being 'really crazy', we should first question the mandates of our own culture and ask ourselves:

- Who are the appearance masters that we feel obliged to serve?

- Do our societal standards have the potential to harm us if we buy into them?

Not everybody exposed to the same cultural and family factors develops a negative body image, suggesting the significance of individual factors in the development of body dissatisfaction. Individual factors may include:

- low self-esteem

- a tendency towards perfectionism

- feelings of a lack of control

- a predisposition to depression or anxiety

- troubled interpersonal relationships.

Andrew Radford (2015), Chief Executive of BEAT (Beating Eating Disorders), told his audience at a recent Public Policy Exchange Symposium Event entitled *Mental Health and Young People: Promoting a Positive and Healthy Body Image* that in his experience body dissatisfaction is closely associated with low self-esteem in children and young people, and he quoted a young person as saying:

> It's [body dissatisfaction] more to do with people being unhappy. We have more pressure to be intelligent, successful and beautiful than ever.

According to Hutchinson and Calland (2011), children develop the majority of their beliefs, attitudes and behaviours from the important adults in their lives. Parents' perceptions of their child's body and the importance they place on their child's looks have a significant impact on how children feel about their own appearance. Parents may knowingly or unwittingly influence their children from infancy either through modelling their own appearance-related anxieties and behaviours, or through their attitudes towards the appearance of their children.

Harter (1999) suggests that by about eight years of age children have internalised the standards and values of those who are important to them, and also by this stage they have developed an appreciation of the values of the society around them. Everyday conversations such as commenting on the appearance of others can communicate the importance parents place on appearance and can create or exacerbate the body image anxieties of their children. While children are strongly influenced by the direct comments that parents make around food, eating and body size and shape, they are also influenced by subtle behaviours or more indirect comments. Children who have mothers who diet and constantly talk about food, calories and body size are more likely to develop issues around their bodies at very early ages.

In today's media-driven culture, as Kater (2004, p.36) writes, messages about looks are routinely delivered to children without discrimination. These messages instruct children about what look they 'supposedly' should have to be desirable and happy. Some of these messages are specifically aimed at 'the *body* that is needed to achieve that look and *what to do* to get that body'. Kater writes that not only are these directives frequently 'at odds with our basic biological nature and conflict with what is needed for physical and emotional well-being…it is also never explained to children that nearly all these media messages exist to make money for someone'.

Children's limited life experience and their level of intellectual development mean that they are unlikely to be aware that the standards of beauty portrayed by the traditional media, i.e. television, films, music, magazines and advertising, contain unrealistic, idealised and stereotypical portrayals of body types. Hutchinson and Calland (2011, p.2) comment:

> Television, mobile phones, magazines, computers and advertising bill-boards bombard us constantly with images of slim and beautiful people and because of the media's powerful presence in our lives we see more images of people every day than we do real faces of family and friends… This has had the effect of making exceptional good looks seem normal, real and achievable.

Research by Knobloch-Westerwick and Crane (2012) suggests that girls who are constantly exposed to media images that promote a thin-as-ideal body have increased dissatisfaction with their own body, and the longer that they are exposed to these types of images, the more dissatisfied they become and the more likely they are to report being on a diet. Even brief exposure to the typical, idealised images of women that we see every day has been shown to lower girls' opinion of themselves both physically and academically (Hargreaves and Tiggemann 2003). This was found to be the case even among girls who were already thin with low body mass indexes, as well as with very young girls.

A report by the American Psychological Association (2007) indicates that the 'girlie-girl' culture's emphasis on beauty and play-sexiness can increase girls' vulnerability to the pitfalls that most concern parents: depression, eating disorders, body dissatisfaction and risky sexual behaviour. It suggested that girls' self-objectification – judging your body by how you think it looks to others – accounted for half the differential in girls' reports of depression and more than two-thirds of the variance in their self-esteem.

For boys, traditional media places an emphasis on fitness and muscularity. Research by Common Sense Media (2015) found that body ideals for boys have become increasingly unattainable over the years, emphasising muscularity wherever it is possible to do so and to boys of younger and younger ages.

DISABILITY

The images of perfection and associated lack of representation of children with disabilities in the media are highly excluding for the population of children and young people with disabilities. On the few occasions that they do feature in the media, Hutchinson and Calland (2011) note that the emphasis is on their disability and they are portrayed as being helpless and needing protection, or alternatively it is on how they have beaten the odds.

A study (MacConville 2007) that I conducted in the London Borough of Ealing explored the social challenges of children with disabilities in mainstream schools. The children I interviewed were clear that the visible differences in their appearances due to unusual physical characteristics or equipment such as hearing aids, crutches, wheelchairs or visual prostheses (for example, glass eye) were disturbing to others. Differences in appearance affecting the eyes to the mouth region – 'the communication triangle' – were reported to be particularly unsettling, and the children said that they constantly received stares and were asked intrusive personal questions that provoked strong feelings of shame, humiliation and frustration, which were clearly damaging to the children's well-being.

The amount of staring and loss of anonymity endured by children who look different should not be underestimated. What emerged from listening to the children in the study was an appreciation of the enormous amount of energy that they expend in school in order to contain their painful feelings and appear 'normal'. They do not want to be found out and are continually engaged in working out how much demand they can make on the school situation without drawing attention to their disability. Allan (1999, p.47) refers to this behaviour as the 'constant policing of the boundaries around themselves' and suggests that the constant imperative to appear 'normal', yet at the same time experiencing significant difficulties, gives a quality of 'undecidability' to those with whom they come into contact. This means that these young people become somewhat anonymous in school and are isolated from the social milieu.

The reality is that children and young people take 'coolness' very seriously because it is a code which helps them to navigate through school with their self-esteem intact. The strict code of cool usually boils down to the common denominator of looking 'right', wearing the 'right' brands and listening to the 'right' music. Children with disabilities can, for a variety of reasons, find it difficult to access these finely tuned rules of cool. They therefore tend to stand out from their peers and are at risk of being socially excluded.

THE ALL PARTY PARLIAMENTARY GROUP (APPG) ON BODY IMAGE

Aiming to raise awareness of the issues surrounding body image dissatisfaction and take forward a campaign to change attitudes and confront the causes of body dissatisfaction, the APPG on Body Image, led by equalities minister Jo Swinson, was formed in 2011 in response to a growing concern about the negative effects of body dissatisfaction on the national self-esteem. The subsequent report released by the Equalities Office, *Reflections on Body Image* (APPG 2012), outlined the key findings and proposed a number of recommendations to tackle body dissatisfaction. The three-month-long inquiry found that 34 per cent of boys and 49 per cent of girls have been on a diet to change their body shape or to lose weight, 42 per cent of girls consider that the most negative part about being female is the pressure to look attractive, and from about the age of five, children begin to recognise that certain body types are more acceptable in society than others. Overall the inquiry found that children and young people are particularly vulnerable to social and cultural pressures to conform to unrealistic beauty ideals.

The inquiry proposed that although children's cognitive abilities have remained fairly constant over time, the beauty ideals that form the basis on which they are judging their own appearance and the appearances of others have become far more exacting. Evidence suggested that changes in society might partly explain why increasing numbers of children of primary school age are exhibiting signs of body dissatisfaction. Day after day, children are bombarded with messages from the media and from their peers, as well as countless other sources, telling them they aren't fit enough, smart enough or attractive enough and that they are certainly not thin enough. The inquiry reported that numerous children have adopted the media's warped view on body shape and size by the time they are just five years old, and over half of girls and a quarter of boys think that their peers have body image problems. Evidence submitted to the inquiry by Professor Nichola Rumsey of the Centre for Appearance Research indicates that:

- more than 50 per cent of children who have experienced bullying reported that it was because of their appearance
- between one-third and a half of young girls fear becoming fat and engage in dieting or binge eating
- girls as young as five years old are worried about the way they look and their size
- one-third of young boys aged 8–12 diet to lose weight.

The inquiry found that, overall, children and young people with body image dissatisfaction are less likely to engage in learning, socialise or participate in school activities. Further adverse consequences of body dissatisfaction include:

- the early onset of a range of physical, emotional and social problems; individuals with body image dissatisfaction are less likely to value their body or prioritise their health and are more likely to engage in unhealthy behaviours
- the onset of depression and eating disorders
- low self-confidence and, as a consequence, a lack of enthusiasm and unwillingness to take part in school activities, sport and exercise or socialise with friends
- wider problems such as teenage pregnancy, drug and alcohol abuse, and youth unemployment.

The inquiry concluded that body dissatisfaction among children and young people is high and on the increase, and for many is now the biggest single worry. It strongly recommended that society must act now in order to safeguard future generations. Although body image dissatisfaction has many causes, it is clear from the outcomes of the inquiry that the media, advertising and our celebrity culture together account for almost three-quarters of the negative influence on body image. In terms of solutions, the report recommended 'mandatory body-image and self-esteem' lessons and that all children develop media literacy skills, as these can play a significant role in promoting body confidence.

BUILDING RESILIENCE

A way forward to ensure that children and young people flourish and maintain and celebrate their innate positive body esteem requires that they have the inner strength to deal successfully with the challenges and demands that they will inevitably encounter. Step forward positive psychologists Robert Brooks and Sam Goldstein (2001, 2013), who call this capacity to flourish *resilience*. Their example speaks to parents and educators who increasingly see the world as a hostile place and who think that the solution is to construct tighter boundaries around children and young people in order to keep out a toxic culture. This solution, these psychologists believe, and I concur, is unrealistic. Our role is not to keep the world at bay but to prepare children so that they can thrive within it. We can only shield children by enabling them to become resilient and have a robust identity and healthy self-esteem because of their strengths and achievements.

If children are to be resilient, not only must they perceive that they have strengths or what Brooks and Goldstein (2001, 2003) call 'Islands of Competence', they must also believe that their strengths are appreciated and supported by the significant adults in their lives. Such adults have been called 'charismatic adults' by the late psychologist Julius Segal – that is, individuals who can help children to gather strengths by enabling them to feel valued and appreciated.

The quality of resilience that can be fostered by such adults is described by Brooks and Goldstein (2001, p.1) as

> the ability of a child to deal more effectively with stress and pressure, to cope with everyday challenges, to bounce back from disappointment and adversity…to develop clear and realistic goals, to solve problems, to relate comfortably with others and to treat oneself with respect…

Resilience is far more common than we might expect. It is not limited to the most able individuals. In his book *The Marshmallow Test*, Walter Mischel (2014), one of the most influential psychologists of the twentieth century, writes that one of the best things that we can do to enable children to become resilient is to model what we would like them to become. How parents and other key figures in children's lives control themselves, how they deal with stress, frustration and emotions, the standards they use in assessing their own achievements, their empathy and sensitivity to other people's feelings, their attitudes, goals and values, their disciplinary strategies and their lack of discipline all influence the child.

Key adults can do much to create the conditions in which children succeed. One important strategy involves working with them on enjoyable but challenging tasks that become increasingly difficult. The challenge is for adults to provide the support that children need to enable them to do the 'heavy lifting' on their own without taking over and doing it for them. Experiences of early success enable children to develop optimistic, reality-based expectations of achievement and enable them to discover for themselves the kinds of activities that ultimately become intrinsically motivating for them.

We can also help children to develop growth mindsets in which they think of their talents, abilities, intelligence and social behaviour not as fixed inborn traits but as skills and competencies that they can cultivate if they invest the effort. As Carol Dweck's (2000, 2006) research illustrates, guiding children to think about their abilities and intelligence as malleable prepares them to use effort to improve their performance.

The purpose of the Positive Body Image curriculum is to prevent children falling prey to the all-pervasive media machine that promotes the unquestioned belief that how they look is more important than who they are, and to provide alternative messages that will enable them to flourish. Our society's celebration of seemingly perfect people will not change overnight; however, strong adult messages can stop children from berating themselves for not having the right appearance and from compromising their health and emotional well-being. Children need to know that nobody has the right to tell them who they're supposed to be or what they're supposed to look like. Young people's potential is endless, and if we can nurture their strengths and a resilient mindset there is no limit to what they can achieve. We need to celebrate the unique individuals that they are and, even more importantly, enable our children to celebrate themselves.

CHAPTER 2

THE PURPOSE OF THIS RESOURCE AND LINKS TO THE CURRICULUM

The purpose of this chapter is to describe the contribution that the Positive Body Image programme makes to schools' statutory responsibilities. Maintained schools have duties under the Children's Act 2004 to promote children's well-being and statutory responsibilities to provide a curriculum that is broadly based, balanced and meets the needs of all pupils.

Under Section 78 of the Education Act 2002 and the Academies Act 2010, such a curriculum must:

- promote the spiritual, moral, cultural, mental and physical development of pupils at the school and of society

- prepare pupils at the school for the opportunities, responsibilities and experiences of later life.

Recent studies highlight the link between health, well-being and educational attainment. Key findings from the evidence highlights that:

- pupils with better health and well-being are likely to achieve better academically

- effective social and emotional competencies are associated with greater health and well-being and better achievement

- a positive association exists between academic attainment and physical activity levels.

SPIRITUAL, MORAL, SOCIAL AND CULTURAL (SMSC) DEVELOPMENT

As of November 2014, every school in England must promote spiritual, moral, social and cultural (SMSC) development and must also show how well their pupils develop in SMSC. SMSC topics should be taught through the National Curriculum and through well-planned personal, social, health and economic education (PSHE).

SMSC is essential for children and young people's individual development, as well as the development of society as a whole.

SMSC has been part of education since the 1944 Education Act and was around in earlier forms before that. It can sum up what a good school is all about – preparing children and young people to live full, active lives as part of their community and into adulthood. Most school mission and value statements have a strong emphasis on SMSC and reflect the values that express some of its core elements. These may include, for example, aspirations to be a safe, happy school where children and young people can fulfil their potential and appreciate others.

Ofsted

Ofsted highlights the importance of SMSC as being central to the development and growth of pupils as people and at the heart of what teachers would say education is all about (Ofsted 2004).

Ofsted inspectors visiting a school always report on the quality of teaching and leadership. They are also looking for something extra – to consider children and young people's SMSC development. Since September 2015 this position has been referenced throughout the Ofsted Inspection Handbook. SMSC is now a key area of inspection, and underdeveloped SMSC provision will affect Ofsted's evaluation of a school's overall effectiveness:

- An outstanding school will have a 'thoughtful and wide-ranging promotion of pupils' spiritual, moral, social and cultural development'.

- An inadequate school will have 'serious weaknesses in the overall promotion of pupils' spiritual, moral, social and cultural development'.

The table below has been designed to enable teachers to reference how the Positive Body Image programme contributes to the development of SMSC, the National Curriculum and the PSHE Programme of Study (2014).

Positive Body Image links to the National Curriculum, PSHE Association's Programme of Study 2014 and Ofsted Framework 2015

Session 1: Introduction to the Positive Body Image programme	
Subject	**Key Stage 2**
National Curriculum: English (spoken language – Years 1–6)	Participate in discussions, presentations, performances, role-play, improvisations and debates. In Years 3 and 4, pupils should become more familiar with and confident in using language in a greater variety of situations, for a variety of audiences and purposes, including drama, formal presentations and debate.
	Demonstrate emotional literacy.
PSHE Association Programme of Study 2014	
Core theme 1: Health and well-being	Learn what positively and negatively affects their physical, mental and emotional health.
Core theme 2: Relationships	Share their opinions on things that matter to them and explain their views through discussions with one other person and the whole class.
	Develop skills to form and maintain positive and healthy relationships.
	Work collaboratively towards shared goals.
Core theme 3: Living in the wider world	Learn why and how rules that protect themselves and others are made and enforced, why different rules are needed in different situations, and how to take part in making and changing rules.
Ofsted Framework 2015 Spiritual development	Show a sense of enjoyment and fascination in learning about themselves, others and the world around them.
	Use imagination and creativity in their learning and willingness to reflect on their experiences.

Session 2: Build your bounce back muscles	
Subject	**Key Stage 2**
National Curriculum: English (spoken language – Years 1–6)	Participate in discussions, presentations, performances, role-play, improvisations and debates. In Years 3 and 4, pupils should become more familiar with and confident in using language in a greater variety of situations, for a variety of audiences and purposes, including drama, formal presentations and debate
PSHE Association Programme of Study 2014	
Core theme 1: Health and well-being	Reflect on and celebrate their achievements, identify their strengths and areas for improvement, and set high aspirations.
Core theme 2: Relationships	Develop skills to form and maintain positive and healthy relationships. Work collaboratively towards shared goals.
Ofsted Framework 2015 Spiritual development	Show a sense of enjoyment and fascination in learning about themselves, others and the world around them. Use imagination and creativity in their learning and willingness to reflect on their experiences.
Social development	Use a range of social skills in different contexts, for example working and socialising with other pupils, including those from different religious, ethnic and socio-economic backgrounds.

Session 3: Strengths spotting	
Subject	**Key Stage 2**
National Curriculum: English (spoken language – Years 1–6)	Participate in discussions, presentations, performances, role-play, improvisations and debates. In Years 3 and 4, pupils should become more familiar with and confident in using language in a greater variety of situations, for a variety of audiences and purposes, including drama, formal presentations and debate. Demonstrate emotional literacy.
PSHE Association Programme of Study 2014	
Core theme 1: Health and well-being	Reflect on and celebrate their achievements, identify their strengths and areas for improvement, and set high aspirations.
Core theme 2: Relationships	Work collaboratively towards shared goals.
Ofsted Framework 2015	Develop skills to form and maintain positive and healthy relationships (Core theme 2).
Spiritual development	Show a sense of enjoyment and fascination in learning about themselves, others and the world around them. Use imagination and creativity in their learning and willingness to reflect on their experiences.
Social development	Use a range of social skills in different contexts, for example working and socialising with other pupils, including those from different religious, ethnic and socio-economic backgrounds.

Session 4: Here and now	
Subject	Key Stage 2
National Curriculum: English (spoken language – Years 1–6)	Participate in discussions, presentations, performances, role-play, improvisations and debates. In Years 3 and 4, pupils should become more familiar with and confident in using language in a greater variety of situations, for a variety of audiences and purposes, including drama, formal presentations and debate.
PSHE Association Programme of Study 2014	
Core theme 2: Relationships	Develop skills to form and maintain positive and healthy relationships.
Ofsted Framework 2015	
Spiritual development	Show a sense of enjoyment and fascination in learning about themselves, others and the world around them.
	Use imagination and creativity in their learning and willingness to reflect on their experiences.
Social development	Use a range of social skills in different contexts, for example working and socialising with other pupils, including those from different religious, ethnic and socio-economic backgrounds.

Session 5: The real you	
Subject	Key Stage 2
National Curriculum: English (spoken language – Years 1–6)	Participate in discussions, presentations, performances, role-play, improvisations and debates. In Years 3 and 4, pupils should become more familiar with and confident in using language in a greater variety of situations, for a variety of audiences and purposes, including drama, formal presentations and debate.
	Demonstrate emotional literacy.
PSHE Association Programme of Study 2014	
Core theme 2: Relationships	Be aware of different types of relationship, including those between acquaintances, friends and relatives, and families.
	Develop skills to form and maintain positive and healthy relationships.
	Share their opinions on things that matter to them and explain their views through discussions with one other person and the whole class.
Ofsted Framework School Inspection Handbook, 2015 Cultural	Understand and appreciate the wide range of cultural influences that have shaped their own heritage and those of others.

Session 6: Healthy eating habits: three to remember	
Subject	Key Stage 2
National Curriculum: Science	Recognise the impact of diet on the way their bodies function (Year 6).
	Research different food groups of the Eatwell Plate, healthy eating and design a healthy school meal.
Design and technology: Cooking and nutrition	Understand and apply the principles of a healthy and varied diet (healthy eating).

National Curriculum: English (spoken language – Years 1–6)	Participate in discussions, presentations, performances, role-play, improvisations and debates. In Years 3 and 4, pupils should become more familiar with and confident in using language in a greater variety of situations, for a variety of audiences and purposes, including drama, formal presentations and debate.
PSHE Association Programme of Study 2014	
Core theme 1: Health and well-being	Recognise opportunities to make their own choices about food, what might influence their choices and the benefits of a balanced diet.
Core theme 2: Relationships	Develop skills to form and maintain positive and healthy relationships. Know how to make informed choices (including recognising that choices can have positive, neutral and negative consequences) and begin to understand the concept of a 'balanced lifestyle'.
Ofsted Framework School Inspection Handbook, 2015	
Moral development	Understand the consequences of their behaviour and actions.

Session 7: Get moving

Subject	Key Stage 2
National Curriculum: English (spoken language – Years 1–6)	Participate in discussions, presentations, performances, role-play, improvisations and debates. In Years 3 and 4, pupils should become more familiar with and confident in using language in a greater variety of situations, for a variety of audiences and purposes, including drama, formal presentations and debate.
Science/PE	Recognise the impact of exercise, on the way their bodies function.
Physical education	Compare their performances with previous ones and demonstrate improvements to achieve their personal best. Enjoy communicating, collaborating and competing with each other. They should develop an understanding of how to improve in different physical activities and sports and how to evaluate and recognise their own success.
PSHE Association Programme of Study 2014	
Core theme 1: Health and well-being	Know how to make informed choices (including recognising that choices can have positive, neutral and negative consequences) and begin to understand the concept of a healthy and 'balanced lifestyle'.
Core theme 2: Relationships	Develop skills to form and maintain positive and healthy relationships.
Ofsted Framework School Inspection Handbook, 2015	
Spiritual	Show a sense of enjoyment and fascination in learning about themselves and others.
Cultural	Demonstrate a willingness to participate in and respond positively to artistic, musical, sporting and cultural opportunities.

Session 8: Have fun	
Subject	**Key Stage 2**
National Curriculum: English (spoken language Years 1–6)	Participate in discussions, presentations, performances, role-play, improvisations and debates.
	Develop skills to form and maintain positive and healthy relationships (Core theme 2).
PSHE	
PSHE Association Programme of Study 2014	
Core theme 1: Health and well-being	Know how to make informed choices (including recognising that choices can have positive, neutral and negative consequences) and begin to understand the concept of a 'balanced lifestyle'.
Core theme 2: Relationships	Work collaboratively towards shared goals.
Ofsted Framework	
School Inspection Handbook, 2015	
Cultural	Demonstrate a willingness to participate in and respond positively to artistic, musical, sporting and cultural opportunities.

Session 9: Television turnoff	
Subject	**Key Stage 2**
National Curriculum: English (spoken language – Years 1–6)	Participate in discussions, presentations, performances, role-play, improvisations and debates.
Maths	Interpret and present data.
PSHE Association Programme of Study 2014	
Core theme 1: Health and well-being	Know how to make informed choices (including recognising that choices can have positive, neutral and negative consequences) and begin to understand the concept of a 'balanced lifestyle'.
Core theme 2: Relationships	Develop skills to form and maintain positive and healthy relationships (Core theme 2).
Ofsted Framework	
School Inspection Handbook, 2015	
Spiritual	Show a sense of enjoyment and fascination in learning about themselves, others and the world around them.
Cultural	Demonstrate a willingness to participate in and respond positively to artistic, musical, sporting and cultural opportunities.

Session 10: Think twice	
Subject	**Key Stage 2**
National Curriculum: English (spoken language – Years 1–6)	Participate in discussions, presentations, performances, role-play, improvisations and debates. In Years 3 and 4, pupils should become more familiar with and confident in using language in a greater variety of situations, for a variety of audiences and purposes, including drama, formal presentations and debate. Demonstrate emotional literacy.
PSHE Association Programme of Study 2014	
Core theme 1: Health and well-being	Learn what positively and negatively affects their physical, mental and emotional health. Deepen their understanding of good and not so good feelings, and extend their vocabulary to enable them to explain both the range and intensity of feelings to others. Understand that pressure to behave in an unacceptable, unhealthy or risky way can come from a variety of sources, including the people they know and the media.
Core theme 2: Relationships	Develop skills to form and maintain positive and healthy relationships. Know how to make informed choices (including recognising that choices can have positive, neutral and negative consequences) and begin to understand the concept of a 'balanced lifestyle'.
Ofsted Framework School Inspection Handbook, 2015	
Spiritual	Show a sense of enjoyment and fascination in learning about themselves, others and the world around them.

Session 11: Pictures, pictures everywhere!	
Subject	**Key Stage 2**
National Curriculum: English (spoken language – Years 1–6)	Participate in discussions, presentations, performances, role-play, improvisations and debates. In Years 3 and 4, pupils should become more familiar with and confident in using language in a greater variety of situations, for a variety of audiences and purposes, including through drama, formal presentations and debate.
	Demonstrate emotional literacy.
PSHE Association Programme of Study 2014	
Core theme 1: Health and well-being	Learn what positively and negatively affects their physical, mental and emotional health, including the media.
	Recognise how images in the media do not always reflect reality and can affect how people feel about themselves.
Core theme 2: Relationships	Develop skills to form and maintain positive and healthy relationships.
	Work collaboratively towards shared goals.
Ofsted Framework School Inspection Handbook, 2015	
Cultural	Understand and appreciate the wide range of cultural influences that have shaped their own heritage and those of others.

Session 12: Thought catching	
Subject	**Key Stage 2**
National Curriculum: English (spoken language – Years 1–6)	Participate in discussions, presentations, performances, role-play, improvisations and debates. In Years 3 and 4, pupils should become more familiar with and confident in using language in a greater variety of situations, for a variety of audiences and purposes, including drama, formal presentations and debate.
PSHE Association Programme of Study 2014	
Core theme 2: Relationships	Develop skills to form and maintain positive and healthy relationships.
	Know how to make informed choices (including recognising that choices can have positive, neutral and negative consequences) and begin to understand the concept of a 'balanced lifestyle'.
	Deepen their understanding of good and not so good feelings, and extend their vocabulary to enable them to explain both the range and intensity of their feelings to others.
	Recognise that they may experience conflicting emotions and when they might need to listen to their emotions or overcome them.
Ofsted Framework School Inspection Handbook, 2015	
Spiritual	Use imagination and creativity in their learning and willingness to reflect on their experiences.
Moral	Understand the consequences of their behaviour and actions.

Session 13: My ABC	
Subject	**Key Stage 2**
National Curriculum: English (spoken language – Years 1–6)	Participate in discussions, presentations, performances, role-play, improvisations and debates. In Years 3 and 4, pupils should become more familiar with and confident in using language in a greater variety of situations, for a variety of audiences and purposes, including drama, formal presentations and debate.
PSHE Association Programme of Study 2014	
Core theme 2: Relationships	Develop skills to form and maintain positive and healthy relationships.
	Know how to make informed choices (including recognising that choices can have positive, neutral and negative consequences) and begin to understand the concept of a 'balanced lifestyle'.
	Deepen their understanding of good and not so good feelings, and extend their vocabulary to enable them to explain both the range and intensity of their feelings to others.
	Recognise that they may experience conflicting emotions and when they might need to listen to their emotions or overcome them.
Ofsted Framework School Inspection Handbook, 2015	
Moral	Use imagination and creativity in their learning and willingness to reflect on their experiences.
	Understand the consequences of their behaviour and actions.

Session 14: How to be a friend

Subject	Key Stage 2
National Curriculum: English (spoken language – Years 1–6)	Participate in discussions, presentations, performances, role-play, improvisations and debates. In Years 3 and 4, pupils should become more familiar with and confident in using language in a greater variety of situations, for a variety of audiences and purposes, including drama, formal presentations and debate.
PSHE Association Programme of Study 2014	
Core theme 2: Relationships	Recognise what constitutes a positive, healthy relationship and develop the skills to form and maintain positive and healthy relationships.
	Recognise ways in which a relationship can be unhealthy and who to talk to if they need support.
	Know how to make informed choices (including recognising that choices can have positive, neutral and negative consequences) and begin to understand the concept of a 'balanced lifestyle'.
	Deepen their understanding of good and not so good feelings, and extend their vocabulary to enable them to explain both the range and intensity of their feelings to others.
	Recognise and respond appropriately to a wider range of feelings in others.
Ofsted Framework School Inspection Handbook, 2015	
Social	Use a range of social skills in different contexts, for example working and socialising with other pupils, including those from different religious, ethnic and socio-economic backgrounds.
Moral	Understand the consequences of their behaviour on others.

Session 15: My hero

Subject	Key Stage 2
National Curriculum: English (spoken language – Years 1–6)	Participate in discussions, presentations, performances, role-play, improvisations and debates. In Years 3 and 4, pupils should become more familiar with and confident in using language in a greater variety of situations, for a variety of audiences and purposes, including drama, formal presentations and debate.
PSHE Association Programme of Study 2014	
Core theme 1: Health and well-being	Learn what positively and negatively affects their physical, mental and emotional health.
Core theme 2: Relationships	Develop skills to form and maintain positive and healthy relationships. Know how to make informed choices (including recognising that choices can have positive, neutral and negative consequences) and begin to understand the concept of a 'balanced lifestyle'.
Ofsted Framework School Inspection Handbook, 2015	
Cultural	Understand and appreciate the wide range of cultural influences that have shaped their own heritage and those of others.
Spiritual	Demonstrate an ability to be reflective about their own beliefs, religious or otherwise, that inform their perspective on life and their interest in and respect for different people's faiths, feelings and values. Show a sense of enjoyment and fascination in learning about themselves, others and the world around them.

Session 16: WOOP

Subject	Key Stage 2
National Curriculum: English (spoken language – Years 1–6)	Participate in discussions, presentations, performances, role-play, improvisations and debates. In Years 3 and 4, pupils should become more familiar with and confident in using language in a greater variety of situations, for a variety of audiences and purposes, including drama, formal presentations and debate.
PSHE Association Programme of Study 2014	
Core theme 1: Health and well-being	Know how to make informed choices (including recognising that choices can have positive, neutral and negative consequences) and begin to understand the concept of a 'balanced lifestyle'.
	Recognise opportunities to make their own choices about food, what might influence their choices and the benefits of eating a balanced diet.
	Reflect on and celebrate their achievements, identify their strengths and areas for improvement, and set high aspirations and goals.
Core theme 2: Relationships	Develop skills to form and maintain positive and healthy relationships.
Ofsted Framework School Inspection Handbook, 2015	
Spiritual	Show a sense of enjoyment and fascination in learning about themselves, others and the world around them.
	Use imagination and creativity in their learning and willingness to reflect on their experiences.

CHAPTER 3

GENERAL GUIDANCE ON DELIVERING THE PROGRAMME

The Positive Body Image programme that forms the backbone of this book has been designed to enable children to celebrate their positive body esteem and reinforce the building blocks of healthy living. Throughout the sessions, active learning strategies enable children to:

- understand the building blocks of healthy living

- discover their strengths and talents

- recognise the protective factors that exist in their lives

- interpret events/circumstances in a positive way

- set realistic goals and work towards reaching them.

ACTIVE LEARNING STRATEGIES

Research studies into preventative education and health-related behaviour emphasise that programmes that are based on only giving information (i.e. increasing knowledge) are not effective. However, Herbert and Lohrmann (2011) noted that programmes that incorporate active learning strategies, such as involving children in more than just listening, with less emphasis on facts and more emphasis on developing skills and engaging children in practical activities and focusing their values and attitudes, are more successful. Such activities help to ensure that children develop the practical skills and attributes that enable them to make the best and healthiest choices based on both knowledge *and* understanding. Although throughout the sessions in the Positive Body Image programme children are encouraged to reflect, problem solve and explore different points of view, they are not encouraged to disclose sensitive, personal information about themselves or others.

ABOUT THE PROGRAMME

The programme consists of 16 sessions that can be used with primary-aged children between the ages of seven and eleven years in a range of settings. The programme is grounded in research from the fields of positive psychology, resilience theory and cognitive behaviour therapy. These relatively new fields of enquiry provide scientific evidence of the qualities and skills that contribute to a healthy and flourishing life. The introductions to each of the 16 sessions describe the theory behind the suggested activities and interventions.

The programme has the overall aim of enabling children to understand how acquiring a particular skill advances the overall goal of celebrating their innate body esteem, reinforcing healthy habits and building resilience. The sessions combine a range of teaching styles and active learning techniques and are mainly based on partner and group work and class discussion. It is intended that the programme should be delivered with a sense of fun and celebration. The programme has been trialled and enjoyed by a wide range of primary-aged children in a variety of mainstream and specialist settings.

WAYS THAT THE PROGRAMME CAN BE DELIVERED

The programme can be used flexibly in schools with a class, a group or across the whole school, in a specialist setting such as a nurture group, or in a special school. It can also be delivered to children on an individual basis. The Take Away activities that accompany the sessions are designed to be completed at home, where ideally the activities will be shared with a family member. Chapter six of this book describes the importance of parental involvement in the programme. It is hoped that the practical engagement of family members in the programme will empower children and their families to make positive behaviour changes in relation to the building blocks of healthy living, and in relation to emotional health and building resilience – the foundations on which a positive body image is based.

APPROACHES ON WHICH THE PROGRAMME IS BASED

The programme is based on research findings from three fields of study: positive psychology, resilience and cognitive behaviour therapy. This section provides a necessarily brief introduction to each field, and suggestions for further reading are included at the end of the book.

Positive psychology

Positive psychology is a relatively new field of study that is concerned with subjective well-being, the technical term for happiness. It was introduced in 1998 by psychologist Martin Seligman when he was elected president of the American Psychological Association. Seligman made the case that psychology was good, but not good enough, because it had neglected the study of what makes life worth living. He argued that, alongside studying mental illness, psychologists should also study human well-being, character strengths and human potential. Positive psychology brings scientific rigour to the field of human flourishing. A recurring theme of this new science is that using our strengths taps into the core of who we are as human beings, and it is through our strengths that we can make our greatest contribution. Positive psychology moves away from the within-child deficit model to an approach based on building capacity and enhancing character strengths such as kindness, courage and creativity and virtues such as citizenship, tolerance and responsibility. Its goal, essentially, is to enhance human strengths such as optimism, courage, honesty, self-understanding and interpersonal skills. Positive psychology provides an approach that enables individuals to recognise and use their inner strengths as buffers against setbacks and adversity. The Positive Body Image programme does not teach positive psychology as such but weaves its key findings into how the programme is delivered.

Resilience

A major component of a strengths-based approach is 'resilience'. If children are to be resilient, they must perceive that they have strengths or what Brooks and Goldstein (2013) call 'Islands of Competence'. They must also believe that their strengths are appreciated and supported by the significant adults in their lives. The late psychologist Julius Segal (1988) coined the term 'charismatic adults' to describe the individuals who enable children to recognise their strengths and feel valued and appreciated.

Resilience is far more common than we might expect. It is not limited to the most able individuals. The pioneering investigator into resilience, Anne Masten, writes:

> Resilience does not come from rare and special qualities, but from the everyday magic of ordinary human resources in the minds, brains and bodies of children, their families and in their communities... The conclusion that resilience emerges from ordinary processes offers an optimistic outlook for action... (Masten 2014, p.235)

Resilience is often described as the ability to 'bounce back'; however, this description is inaccurate. Resilient individuals have staying power, and when the going gets tough, they do not react automatically like a spring returning to its rest position. Resilient individuals are not passive – they believe that they can decide things that will make a difference, or they are content to wait but remain optimistic. Essentially, they are able to think in a reflective way, to weigh things up and problem solve in the expectation of a positive outcome. Resilient individuals have a sense of autonomy; they do not feel dependent on others to make things happen. Instead, following a setback they are able to regain their equilibrium using a variety of skills, personal attributes and strategies, usually helped by a charismatic adult such as a reliable parent or other adult who is able to reinforce their self-belief and realistic optimism.

Cognitive behaviour therapy

Cognitive behaviour therapy (CBT) is an effective way to help young people deal with their psychological and behavioural difficulties and build resilience (Kazdin and Weisz 1998; Roth and Fonagy 1996; Wallace *et al.* 1995). This is because it has the capacity to reveal the role that our thoughts and beliefs play in relation to both our emotions and our behaviour.

CBT is innovative in the sense that there is no focus on the past as there is with traditional psychotherapy; instead it focuses on ways to improve an individual's state of mind in the here and now. It is being increasingly recognised that many of the mental health issues that young people suffer are because they are frequently flooded with anxious and negative thoughts. If unchecked, these thoughts can reinforce a state of inadequacy, low self-esteem and a lack of confidence. CBT can help young people to reframe their negative thoughts and beliefs and see how these are affecting their feelings and also their behaviour.

Clearly this process takes practice. It usually follows a process that Seligman (1995) describes in his book *The Optimistic Child* and calls ABC.

The ABC of cognitive behaviour therapy

This approach breaks a particular situation into three smaller parts:

- *A: the activating event.* This is often referred to as the trigger – the thing that causes an individual to have negative thoughts.

- *B: an individual's beliefs.* These can include the thoughts, rules, meanings and assumptions that an individual attaches to both real and imagined events.

- *C: the consequences.* These are the emotions, behaviours and physical sensations accompanying these different beliefs. It is important to explore with young people how the way that they think or their beliefs about the activating event or trigger can affect their feelings, both physically and emotionally.

CBT enables individuals, first, to recognise how these three distinct stages operate in their lives and, second, to work towards an understanding of how revising their beliefs can lead to a more positive interpretation of events.

GETTING THE WHOLE SCHOOL INVOLVED

The outcomes of recent studies (Public Health England 2014; Weichselbaum and Buttriss 2014) suggest that a whole-school approach is best placed to convince children of the importance of a healthy lifestyle. The themes that are addressed throughout the Positive Body Image programme will be of interest to a wider population of children than the class or classes to whom the programme is delivered. This is because it is generally recognised in our society, with its emphasis on celebrity and fashion, that children's worries about their appearance and especially their weight concerns have become almost the norm. Children also face exposure to the media on a far greater scale than ever before. It is important, therefore, that steps are taken to ensure that the learning that takes place in the class where the Positive Body Image programme is delivered is also disseminated throughout the school in order to enable a wider population of children to benefit from its key messages. Suggestions for involving the whole school in the programme include the following:

- Display the ChildLine posters around the school to raise awareness of the confidential, free phone line service that is available to all children and young people.

- The Mind Maps, Draw and Write activities and adverts that children design as part of the Positive Body Image programme could be used as displays on the noticeboards around the school to raise awareness of the topics that are addressed throughout the programme.

- Children could use school assemblies to present learning from the programme, or make presentations to other classes. Topics could include how to make and keep friends, how to have a better conversation, and rules for healthy eating.

- The confidential letter box that is recommended for use in the classes where the programme is delivered could be extended to the rest of the school either by placing a letter box in each classroom or in a central location in the school that can be easily accessed by all children. It will be essential to ensure that if children choose to use the letter box they understand the rules for using it and are fully aware of the limits to its confidentiality.

- The compliment cards that children create for their Talk Partners as part of the programme could be used as a school display. Please see p.57 for a definition of Talk Partners.

- The results of the challenges that children engage in during the programme, such as getting out of their comfort zone, reducing screen time and getting moving, could be celebrated at school assemblies and the associated work used as a display.

- The strengths and talents of the everyday heroes that are explored in the programme could be usefully made into an inspirational display to raise awareness and celebrate the importance of character strengths such as kindness, helpfulness and courage.

SCHEDULING THE PROGRAMME

Studies suggest that long-term programmes are more likely to produce more enduring benefits (Greenberg, Domilrovich and Bunbarger 2001; Greenberg *et al.* 2003; Wells, Barlow and Stewart-Brown 2003). Ideally, therefore, the programme should be delivered in its entirety and the sessions scheduled to be delivered on a regular weekly or fortnightly basis to reinforce learning. Children will benefit from the predictability of knowing when the sessions will take place and can look forward to regular engagement with the programme. It is also important to avoid scheduling the programme for times when individual children are likely to miss parts of the sessions. It can be disappointing for children to start exploring a topic but then not have the opportunity to complete it. Also, as partner and group work is vital to how the programme is delivered, it is disruptive to the overall coherence of the programme for the membership of the class or group to be inconsistent. When practitioners prioritise a regular time slot to deliver the programme, they signal to children its importance.

With the inevitable time pressures on schools, the need for flexibility must be taken into account. The programme has therefore been designed so that each of the 16 sessions can be delivered as standalone resources.

Timings

It is estimated that each session will take approximately 45 minutes to deliver to a mainstream class, with an additional 30 minutes per session for preparation and review. As a whole, based on these approximate timings, the complete programme will require a total of 24 hours to deliver. In specialist settings or when the programme is delivered to a small group or to an individual child, the sessions may take less time to deliver.

The timings that are suggested throughout the sessions are approximate and represent the minimum time that is required to deliver each of the activities. Although it is important for sessions to be delivered at a pace that holds children's interests, it is also essential to ensure that the needs of the class are being met. Thus it may be important at times to spend longer on a certain activity if the children are engaged and working towards the learning outcomes. When this is the case, it may be appropriate to extend the learning across two sessions.

STRUCTURE OF THE SESSIONS

The single most important factor influencing learning is what the learner already knows. Ascertain this and teach accordingly. (Ausubel, Novak and Hanesian 1978, p.47)

The planning stage

To maximise children's involvement in the programme, ideally their involvement needs to start *before* the programme begins. The PSHE Association, Teacher Guidance: Key Standards in teaching about body image (2015, p.3) recommends that when teaching about body image, 'it is important to ensure that it builds on appropriate earlier learning. This is so that it forms part of a developmental, spiral curriculum, where learning is seen as continuous and pupils are given opportunities to revisit and extend on prior learning as appropriate for their age and maturity, rather than being a patchwork quilt of unrelated 'topics'.

At the planning stage, introduce the children to the 'big picture' of the programme, i.e. the themes that will be covered throughout the programme, and ask them for their ideas about *what* and *how* they would like to learn about them and also to suggest relevant, further topics. Feedback from teachers who have trialled the programme reveals that children frequently come up with suggestions that are more relevant and meaningful to them than the ideas from their teachers.

The sessions

Throughout the programme the sessions are based on a three-part structure:

1. Introduction

2. Mid-session learning stop

3. Final plenary.

1. Introduction

EFFECTIVE STARTS TO SESSIONS

Understanding the 'big' picture of the session is important for all learners, so throughout the programme the first moments of each session introduce the focus of the session. Starting a lesson by capturing the children's interest is important in order to get the class instantly engaged. Children need to know the learning objective and learning outcome at the point at which they are engaging with any task on which they will be assessed.

Inevitably children will have existing knowledge, beliefs and misconceptions relating to most of the topics that are covered by the programme. It is important to explore this existing knowledge at the beginning of each session. Starter tasks or baseline assessments are included in every session in order to gauge the children's learning needs and to avoid assuming that what has been planned for the session is appropriate for each learner. By involving children in starter tasks that involve problem solving or explanation tasks, we are engaging them, finding out what they know and also standing the session on its head; instead of teaching followed by task, task is followed by teaching, with the benefit of knowledge and wisdom. Throughout the programme, starter tasks include the following:

- Brainstorming.

- Using photographs or pictures to stimulate discussion.

- 'Draw and Write' activities. These are described by the PSHE Association (2013) as activities in which children are asked to respond to an open-ended question by drawing a picture about a particular issue and writing notes to explain it. Draw and Write activities are useful starter tasks as they provide valuable assessment information about what the children already know about a topic. They also provide useful outcome information when children add to their work at the end of the session using a different colour pen to show new learning and expanded knowledge – new ideas, understanding, attitude change, beliefs, feelings – that they have gained from the session.

- Mind Maps. These provide assessment information about what the children already know about a topic. As with Draw and Write activities, described above, new knowledge and ideas can be added at the end of the session in a different colour pen to indicate new learning.

- Creating a key vocabulary list for each session and exploring the children's understanding of their meanings. The words can be made into cards and distributed for paired or group discussion.

Note: When Draw and Write activities and Mind Maps are used as starter tasks at the beginning of sessions and then revisited in the final, plenary they provide children with opportunities to add the new learning, thoughts and ideas that they have gained during the session. Both these activities therefore provide useful assessment and evaluation data.

2. Mid-session learning stop

Mid-session learning stops are structured into every session. These 'stops' provide a time for partner, group or whole-class discussions and, depending on the task the class are engaged in, an opportunity to work together on 'co-operative marking'.

CO-OPERATIVE MARKING

Co-operative marking involves a teacher randomly selecting a child's piece of work to mark with the class. A visualiser or document camera can make the piece of work visible to the whole class and enable the teacher and the class to analyse it together, identifying its good points and, if necessary, suggesting improvements.

Randomly choosing a child's work for co-operative marking is an important strategy for creating an inclusive classroom. It creates a sense of fairness and also ensures that everybody in the class is focused, as they don't know if their work will be selected. Any child's work – the highest or the lowest achiever – may be chosen for co-operative marking. Throughout the programme the approach to co-operative learning that is described is based on the four-step procedure originally devised by Clarke (2014).

THE FOUR-STEP ROUTINE FOR MID-SESSION LEARNING STOPS

1. Randomly choose a child's work to use for co-operative marking. Make the chosen piece of work visible to the whole class, ideally using a visualiser or document camera if possible. Ask the class to take a few moments to read through the piece of work first or look at it if it is a diagram, a Mind Map or a Draw and Write activity.

2. In pairs, i.e. with their Talk Partner, ask the class to decide what are the best parts of the work. Take feedback from the class and encourage the children to give their views about the 'best bits'. These parts of the work are then underlined and analysed by the class as to why they are good. This may be because they reflect the learning outcome for the session or for other reasons that the class may suggest.

3. The class is then asked if there are any parts of the work that could be improved or made even better. The class may need to be reminded that it is important not to suggest changes if there is no obvious need for improvement in order to leave the work (and the confidence of the learner) intact.

4. After this modelling, children work with their Talk Partner (a randomly chosen peer) and discuss their own work, one piece of work at a time, identifying its good features and discussing possible improvements.

3. Final plenary: ensuring effective endings

Each session ends with a plenary, a review of whether the learning outcomes for the session have been met and a round-up or summary of the learning that has taken place during the session. The use of Talk Partners during this process is recommended in order to increase children's confidence in subsequently sharing their ideas with the class or group.

Strategies that are used in the programme during the final plenary to review children's learning include the following:

• Questioning: asking children 'What did you learn?' Asking what they have learnt enables children to consolidate their learning and reminds them of the point of the lesson. Children can also be asked to select, from everything they learnt in a lesson, the one thing that they felt was most important to them. This can provide important feedback to the teacher, as their answers can include both the knowledge and the skills that they have learnt.

- Tell or ask. Children can be asked to think of one question they have about the lesson – which could be 'What if...?' or 'Next could we...?' It can also provide an opportunity for children to 'tell' if there was an aspect of the session that they didn't understand or would like time to explore in more detail.

- I am proud of... Children can then decide what they are most pleased with about their learning. This can include either the knowledge or process skills that the children have acquired or what they have learnt through working with their Talk Partner, in a group or with the whole class.

- I need to work on... Children identify the areas that they recognise they need to continue work on.

- Adding new learning to Mind Maps and Draw and Write activities from the beginning of the session.

- Closing rounds. Each child describes what they have learnt from the session. These contributions should include both the basic information from the session and aspects of social and emotional learning. The contributions that the children make during the closing rounds should be recorded either by the teacher, another adult or by the children themselves to provide evidence of the learning that has taken place during the session.

TALK PARTNER COMPLIMENT SLIPS

Introduce the class to Talk Partner compliment slips and talk through some suggestions of the qualities and behaviours that they may like to compliment their Talk Partner on. Suggest that they may wish to complete a compliment slip for their Talk Partner when they feel that they have worked well together. The compliment slip should look something like this:

To ....   Date: ....

Thank you for being my Talk Partner today.

You helped me learn because you:

-
-

To be an even better Talk Partner next time, you could:

-
-

Signed: ....

Available at www.jkp.com/voucher using the code MACCONVILLEPOSITIVE

Throughout the programme the sessions involve children engaging in active learning strategies, and this can be emotionally tiring for all involved – both staff and children. Advice from the PSHE Association (2015) suggests that building in a light-hearted activity at the very end of each session can be affirming and a good way to change the class atmosphere so that children are ready for their next lesson. Roffey (2011) recommends that *Pass the smile* can be a useful activity to end a session. The teacher smiles to the person on the left, who then passes the smile to the person on their left, until the smile has travelled all around the class.

Teachers may wish to ensure that they are available for a short time following the session so that if a child has any concerns or found the session in anyway troubling they are able to speak to the teacher in private.

ASSESSMENT AND EVALUATION

The PSHE Association's (2007) guidance on assessment reassures teachers that it is generally recognised that some aspects of social and emotional learning lend themselves more easily to assessment than others. This is because although assessing a child's knowledge of facts is usually relatively straightforward, a child's self-esteem, confidence and sense of identity cannot be assessed so accurately. Advice from the PSHE Association (2016, p.11) suggests that although teachers may not be able to accurately assess these areas, 'pupils will be able to judge for themselves whether they feel more confident, or have a firmer sense of their own beliefs and opinions than they did before'. Although these sorts of judgements that children make themselves are generally not written down, making time within the programme for children to reflect on their progress in these areas either individually or through partner or group discussion is important, and recording their views can provide valuable assessment information.

The PSHE Association (2016) suggests that *ipsative* assessment (Hughes 2011) is an approach that is appropriate for assessing areas of social and emotional learning. This approach compares the children's results against their own previous results, so the standard against which any change in performance is measured is the pupil's own performance, rather than the performance of others or the requirements of an exam syllabus. Within the Positive Body Image programme, assessing children's learning of necessity involves a combination of teacher assessment and pupil self-assessment.

Throughout the programme, assessment and evaluation is an integral part of each session. Assessment refers to determining what a child has learned and what still needs to be learned. This approach is based on the guidance from the PSHE Association (2007, p.10):

> To be successful independent learners, children need regular opportunities to reflect on and identify what they have learnt, what needs to be learnt next and what they need to do to continue their learning. This may be to compare their progress against their own starting point or that of others... Teachers and other professionals also need to be clear about the progress and achievements of the children and young people they teach and how their learning might be improved.

The integrated approach to assessment and evaluation that is used throughout the programme also incorporates the five key factors identified by the QCA (Qualifications and Curriculum Authority 2004, 2005) that are essential for improving learning through assessment:

1. The provision of effective feedback to learners.

2. The active involvement of children in their own learning.

3. Adjusting teaching to take account of the results of the assessment.

4. Recognition of the profound influence assessment has on the motivation and self-esteem of learners.

5. The need for learners to be able to assess themselves and understand how to improve.

The approaches to assessment and evaluation that are suggested throughout the programme are described below.

Learning objectives and learning outcomes

Note: Throughout the programme *learning objectives* refers to what the teacher (or others) intends learners to learn. *Learning outcomes* are what are expected from the learner as a result of a task or session, i.e. how achievement will be demonstrated by the learners (PSHE Association 2007).

A key feature of the programme is that assessment relates closely to specified learning outcomes. Learning objectives and outcomes are explained to the children at an appropriate point towards the beginning of each session, and discussed with them in every session. Sharing the learning objectives and outcomes with the children is crucial to the Positive Body Image approach as it is a way of enabling children to be in control of their learning and enhances their autonomy. Ideally this takes place near the beginning of the sessions, but as noted above not necessarily in the first few moments when it is important to capture the children's interest in the focus of the lesson. Although a time in the sessions for sharing learning objectives and outcomes has been indicated in the session notes, this can be altered to suit the pattern of work in each class. Learning outcomes are reviewed in the final plenary of every session.

Starter tasks/Baseline assessment

The starter tasks described earlier in this chapter provide assessment information that help teachers to:

• identify what is already known

• identify any special needs

• decide where to start the session and guide them in how the work should be developed.

Co-operative marking

Co-operative marking is described earlier in this chapter. This process provides useful assessment feedback to learners during the mid-session learning stops, as it:

- identifies strengths in the children's work and how to develop them further

- identifies weaknesses and how they might be addressed and areas for development

- focuses on the learner rather than the teacher

- motivates learners, because each child becomes a partner in the assessment process.

Giving feedback

The successful and constructive use of Talk Partners and co-operative marking throughout the programme depends on the ability of both teachers and learners to provide skilful and constructive feedback. Guidance from the PSHE Association (2007) suggests that if handled well, feedback can contribute positively to a learner's confidence and self-esteem, as it intrinsically respects their individuality and self-worth. Thus developing the skills of giving constructive feedback contributes to a key aim of the programme – to build children's resilience by enhancing the trust between them and staff members and also their peers. Constructive feedback is more likely to be successful when it takes place in a safe learning environment in which there are negotiated ground rules. According to the PSHE Association (2007), it should:

- be clear, specific and honest

- start with comments on the strengths of the work being assessed before areas of improvement

- be based on specific success criteria, not general impressions

- always end on a positive note of achievement.

Summative assessment

Summative assessment or 'assessment of learning' is any assessment which summarises what has been learnt. Summative assessment is carried out at the end of each session and at the end of the programme. As noted earlier in this chapter, it is important to leave enough time at the end of each session to review the learning outcomes and to consolidate learning so that learners are clear about the point of the session.

Examples of summative assessments that are used in the programme include:

- a true/false quiz to identify what has been learnt and to identify whether there are still any areas of confusion or gaps in learning

- presentations by learners

- before-and-after statements

- Mind Maps

- Draw and Write activities

- closing rounds: 'One new thing I have learnt today...'

End-of-programme evaluation

An evaluation that can be used at the end of the programme in schools and settings where the whole programme has been delivered is reproduced on the following page. It can also be used as an end of session evaluation.

Suggestions for further reading on assessment and evaluation in PSHE are included at the end of the book.

RESOURCES

In addition to the usual writing and drawing materials, the resources that are required for delivering each session are listed at the beginning of the session notes.

Programme log

At the beginning of the programme each child should be provided with a programme log. Ideally this should be an A4 ring file with dividers in which children can keep session notes and completed activity sheets; however, in schools where budgetary considerations mean that this is not possible, folders that the children make themselves from folded A3 art paper and treasury tags can provide a practical alternative. It is helpful for children to be able to keep the activity sheets from each session in one place, as they are frequently asked to refer back to earlier sessions throughout the programme.

Children should be encouraged to take pride in their programme logs and add to them their own personal thoughts and also cuttings from magazines and newspapers which are of particular interest to them and relevant to the programme.

The programme log also provides children with a vehicle in which they can ask general questions about the sessions and to which the teacher can respond with comments and stickers and provide praise and words of encouragement.

Right Now activity sheets

Each session has at least one Right Now activity sheet. These activities offer children opportunities to reinforce the skill or concept being taught. They usually require a small amount of writing or drawing and are completed individually, in pairs or in groups, depending on the task. In most sessions it is suggested that the relevant activity sheet is enlarged to an A3 poster size and placed in a central position in the classroom so that it can be used as a focal point for the lesson.

The activity sheets are intended to be used as starting points to activate children's involvement in the material being presented and spark off responses based on their individual experiences and feelings. Ian Morris (2009) suggests that just reading a worksheet will have little effect: getting the children to practise a new skill and talk and write about it will raise their chances of using that skill more frequently. Unless children have opportunities to relate to the concepts being introduced through active learning strategies rather than simply being passive learners, effective learning will not take place. Children may have an intellectual grasp of the programme's content, but it will not be, in Morris's words, 'embedded in the core of their being'.

Extension activities

Extension activities are provided for most sessions. These have been designed to provide further learning opportunities for those children who complete the Right Now activity well within the suggested timeframe or wish to extend their learning outside the session. Many of these children will be higher achievers.

Take Away activities

Take Away activities are suggested towards the end of each session. These activities have been designed to promote a fuller understanding of the topic by building on and extending what has been introduced in the session. Take Away activities have been designed to be practical and engaging and ensure that the skills and concepts that are introduced in the session are reinforced in everyday situations.

Time should be allocated towards the end of the sessions to ensure that the class understands the Take Away tasks. Collaborative problem solving and enabling children to begin to think through the task in the session can provide them with the confidence that the task is going to be 'do-able'. First, the task needs to be explained to the class, and then by beginning to work through it in the session, children can start to feel confident about what the task involves and about completing it.

Further information: useful websites and recommended reading

As the programme may trigger concerns, it will be important to provide children with information about the sources of help that are available to them both within and outside the school. Children may need guidance in developing the skills that they need in order to be able to ask for advice and express their concerns. A list of useful websites and resources can be found at the end of this book.

FACILITATOR REFLECTION

While popular media that promotes a thin-as-ideal body can play a significant role in how children feel about their appearance, the messages that they receive from parents and teachers are also critically important. The role that key adults have in shaping children's attitudes to their own bodies cannot be overstated. Children learn what is important to adults by listening to them and by watching them. They pay more attention to what we do than what we say. When children hear adults expressing dissatisfaction with their bodies, they may begin to believe that being an adult means being dissatisfied with one's body. And when they hear adults disparaging the bodies of others, they may mimic this behaviour by teasing other children about their appearance. *Teacher Guidance: Key Standards in Teaching About Body Image* (PSHE Association undated, p.9) suggests that it is very easy to slip into:

- fat talk (self-deprecating commentary on our own appearance)

- complimenting people on weight loss

- suggesting that someone's appearance is the most important thing about them

- chatter about unflattering photos of celebrities

- talking negatively about how appearance changes with age.

Although in themselves none of these are problematic in moderation, the problem is that in our culture they are frequently not discussed in moderation, so children are likely to hear these messages numerous times on a daily basis.

It is important, therefore, that teachers who will be delivering the programme are careful that they are not sending mixed messages with respect to body image and ensure that their personal beliefs and views do not influence their teaching. When adults model respect for and acceptance of themselves and others, regardless of body size or other physical attributes, we help children to withstand the pressure of the media culture around them and to embrace their strengths and talents.

Support for teachers who are delivering the programme

A key principle of PSHE education is that there is a positive approach to learning that does not attempt to shock or induce guilt but focuses on what children can do to keep themselves and others healthy and safe. Timothy Wilson (2011), professor in psychology at New York University, calls strategies that set out to shock or frighten children 'scared straight' approaches. He describes how these approaches are invariably unsuccessful in deterring children from engaging in risky or unhealthy behaviours because they undermine children's confidence and self-esteem.

Guidance from the PSHE Association (undated, p.25): suggests that 25 per cent of teachers delivering lessons on body image do not feel confident in providing them. It is important, therefore, that teachers who will be delivering the Positive Body Image programme receive the correct training and support to ensure that they feel confident about delivering the programme.

Training, supervision and support

It is important to ensure that teachers who are responsible for delivering the programme have access to the training which is presented in Chapter four of this book, and access to other appropriate training.

It is also crucial that teachers have access to regular support and supervision. The senior leadership team must therefore ensure that:

- they are fully aware of the programme and are available to be a port of call for any concerned teachers, children or parents

- measures are in place for all members of staff, especially those who will be delivering the programme, to attend the training that is described in Chapter four of this book

- regular supervision and debriefing sessions are provided for members of staff who have responsibility for delivering the programme

- there is a port of call for any concerned teachers.

CONFIDENTIALITY, SAFEGUARDING AND HOW TO HANDLE DISCLOSURES

Schools have statutory responsibilities for safeguarding and well-being under the Children Act 2004. Teachers should always work within the school's policies on safeguarding and confidentiality when delivering the programme.

Safeguarding in schools is more than simply keeping children safe. We leave children vulnerable if we do not do everything we can to equip them to keep *themselves* safe in school, outside school and in the future (PSHE Association 2014). The Positive Body Image programme contributes to the safeguarding agenda by supporting the development of children's resilience and self-confidence. Throughout the programme, active learning strategies enable children to explore what makes a respectful relationship and how to make and keep friends. They encourage children to become familiar with the key skills of CBT such as reframing negative thinking patterns and understanding the connection between their thoughts, beliefs and behaviour, and using these skills in their day-to-day lives. Children's competency in media literacy is also increased.

When delivering the programme, teachers should establish a safe teaching and learning environment by:

- agreeing appropriate ground rules with the class (this process is explored on page 54 of this book)

- distancing or depersonalising the learning

- not focusing on individual pupils' circumstances

- providing a confidential letter box in the classroom so that children can ask questions anonymously before, after or during the lesson

- signposting to sources of one-to-one confidential support and ensuring that children have the practical skills to be able to access these services

- going beyond giving information and raising awareness, and focusing on the active learning strategies that enable children to develop healthy habits and the skills that they need to make safe choices.

Distancing techniques

Due to the personal nature of the programme and the fact that it is a curriculum subject, not a therapeutic intervention, the learning should be 'distanced from the learner'. Although self-reflection is vital when children are learning about topics such as the building blocks of healthy living and positive body image, and these topics are best explored within a framework that employs active learning strategies and is relevant to children's lives, creating emotional distance is vital. Distancing creates an 'emotional space' between pupils and the issue that is being explored, thus preventing the sessions becoming too personal. Role-play, for example, can be used to enable pupils to explore, rehearse and develop risk-management and decision-making skills in a safe environment. Distancing also helps to avoid embarrassment and protects pupils' privacy by depersonalising the learning (DfEE 2000). Useful strategies include using:

- case studies and scenarios

- role-play and storyboarding

- puppets

- short film clips.

Although case studies and short videos can work well, teachers should consider them very carefully, in good time ahead of the lesson, to ensure that they do not reflect the circumstances of any of the children in the class.

Children can be encouraged to provide advice to the characters in these fictional scenarios. Advice from the PSHE Association (2015, p.18) suggests that children's exploration of 'something happening to someone else' is very different from talking about themselves and exploring their own feelings and experiences. It is essential that any personal disclosures are supported in a safe context *outside* the main lesson.

Body image is by definition a personal topic, in which children need to reflect on their own strengths, talents, attitudes and intrapersonal and interpersonal skills in order to enhance their self-esteem and draw their attention to the protective factors that exist in their lives. However, care should also be taken in this context that this learning takes place in a distanced way and that children are only asked to reflect on their strengths and the protective factors in their lives when it is safe to do so and without being 'put on the spot' (PSHE 2015).

Disclosures

It is also important that children understand school policies on the disclosure of confidential information, and it is always essential to be clear and honest with a child about the limits of confidentiality. If you are worried about a child being at risk in any way, it is important to speak, as soon as possible, to the appropriate member of staff. This will usually be the lead member of staff for safeguarding or the child protection officer.

Handling disclosures

If a child comes to you and makes a disclosure, it's important to be aware that sharing this information usually takes a great deal of courage. Children often have to grapple with a lot of issues, including the fear that no one will believe them. Care must be taken to remain calm and to show support to the child throughout the disclosure phase. The following four-step process for handling disclosures, which gives the Receive, Reassure, React and Record guidelines recommended by the British Council, will help to lessen the risk of causing more disturbance to the child and in some circumstances compromising a criminal investigation during the disclosure phase.

Receive:

Listen to what is being said without displaying shock or disbelief. A common reaction to unpleasant or even shocking news is denial. However, if you display denial to a child, or show shock or disgust at what they are saying, the child may be afraid to continue and will shut down. Accept what is being said without judgement. Take it seriously.

Reassure:

- Reassure the child, but only so far as is honest and reliable. Don't make promises that you can't be sure to keep.

- Reassure the child that they did nothing wrong and that you take what is said seriously.

- Don't promise confidentiality – never agree to keep secrets. You have a duty to report your concerns.

- Tell the child that you will need to tell some people, but only those whose job it is to protect children.

- Acknowledge how difficult it must have been to talk. It takes a lot for a child to come forward.

React:

- Listen quietly, carefully and patiently. Do not assume anything – don't speculate or jump to conclusions.

- Don't investigate, interrogate or decide if the child is telling the truth. Cases of an allegation of child abuse may lead to a criminal investigation, so don't do anything that may jeopardise a police investigation. Let the child explain to you in their own words what happened, but don't ask leading questions.

- Do ask open questions like 'Is there anything else that you want to tell me?'

- Communicate with the child in a way that is appropriate to their age, understanding and preference. This is especially important for children with disabilities and for children whose preferred language is not English.

- Do not ask the child to repeat what they have told you to another member of staff.

- Explain what you have to do next and whom you have to talk to.

- Refer directly to the named child protection officer in your school.

- Do not discuss the case with anyone else.

Record:

- Make some very brief notes at the time and write them up in detail as soon as possible.

- Do not destroy your original notes in case they are required by the court.

- Record the date, time and place, the words used by the child, and how the child appeared to you – be specific. Record the actual words used, including any swear words or slang.

- Record statements and observable things, not your interpretations or assumptions – keep it factual.

(British Council, n.d.)

HOW TO CREATE A SAFE AND POSITIVE LEARNING ENVIRONMENT

This section explores the main elements that are vital to the creation of a safe and positive learning environment so that effective social and emotional learning can take place. According to the PSHE Association (2015), the three pillars of this are:

- establishing ground rules with pupils

- using 'distancing' techniques (these were described earlier)

- knowing how to deal with unexpected questions or comments.

Although the programme is written according to a strengths-based approach and emphasises the building blocks of healthy living, it is important that teachers are aware that the subject matter may still be deeply sensitive for some children, their parents and also for members of staff. In terms of delivering the sessions it is inevitable that at some point during the programme children will raise sensitive issues. As the PSHE Association (2012) guidance emphasises, it is important that teachers establish and maintain a safe teaching and learning classroom and create a climate of trust, co-operation and support. A safe environment enables open discussion to take place and helps to make sure that teachers are not anxious about unexpected disclosures or comments. A safe environment also encourages children to share feelings, explore attitudes, express opinions and think about those of others with confidence, safe in the knowledge that they will not receive negative feedback.

Suggestions for creating a safe classroom environment include the following:

- Working with pupils to establish ground rules about how children will behave towards each other in discussion and throughout the sessions.

- Making a confidential letter box available in the classroom throughout the programme to enable children to ask questions that they may feel uncomfortable asking in front of their peers and thus to ensure that they do not have to raise these sensitive issues openly in the classroom. This confidential letter box should also be available prior to, during and after the sessions. Providing a way of enabling pupils to ask questions prior to the sessions can inform lesson planning based on children's current needs and understanding. The children's questions can also provide a source of information about where safeguarding/pastoral issues may exist which need following up.

Teachers must also know how to deal with unexpected questions or comments from children. They need to be aware that when they are delivering the programme they are in an influential position and must work within the school's values. Teachers therefore have a particular responsibility to consider how far they should express their own views. They also need to:

- be sensitive to the particular needs and feelings of some pupils who may have direct experience of some of the issues

- always work with the school's policies on safeguarding and confidentiality, ensuring that children understand school policies on disclosure of confidential information and following up concerns in a more appropriate setting outside the classroom

- make pupils aware of sources of support both inside and outside school and ensure that they have the practical skills to be able to access the support

- link the programme to PSHE education and to the whole-school approach to supporting pupil welfare.

A safe learning environment that encourages open and honest discussion should not include discussion about one's own or others' personal lives. General situations should be used as examples, but not names that could identify anyone or cause anybody to be embarrassed or 'put on the spot'.

Establishing ground rules

It is important that throughout the programme discussion takes place in an environment of trust, co-operation and support. When teaching areas that are directly about the children themselves, it is important to take into account the likelihood of disclosures from pupils. Although disclosures should be viewed as a positive impact of the learning, it is important that if children do make disclosures to school staff that they are made in a suitable one-to-one situation. It is not appropriate to encourage children to discuss sensitive, personal matters in the classroom. Before teaching about body image, clear ground rules should be established. To be effective, ground rules should always be negotiated with the class so that children share ownership of them and recognise their relevance. Teachers may, however, need to steer the process and make suggestions to ensure that important considerations are included. Examples of these factors include:

- not asking personal questions

- respecting what others say

- listening to others

- having the right to remain silent if you do not wish to comment.

It is suggested that ground rules are agreed with the class in the first session of the programme and that they are:

- revisited at the beginning of every subsequent session and maintained or updated

- written in the children's own words

- displayed in the classroom

- signed by the children like a contract

- consistently adhered to by the teacher and children.

By being involved in agreeing rules, children no longer feel that they are subject to an arbitrary authority but understand the purpose of rules and take responsibility for them because they have contributed to their development. Children who perceive that they have a degree of autonomy in the classroom are more likely to be intrinsically motivated and fully engaged in learning than those who experience the classroom climate as controlling (Ryan and Deci 2000; Thuen and Bru 2009; Wang and Zollers 1990).

The PSHE Association (2013) recommends that ground rules could usefully include the following:

- not asking personal questions

- respecting what other people say

- listening to others

- having the right to 'pass' if you do not want to comment.

Asking questions

Throughout the programme it is important to ensure that there is a secure classroom environment where children feel safe to ask questions and explore their initial ideas about a topic. As described earlier in this chapter, making a confidential letter box available in the classroom is a useful way of ensuring that pupils have a safe way of asking questions that they may feel shy or embarrassed about asking openly in the classroom.

Supporting vulnerable pupils

It is important to take into account the particular needs of individual pupils who are likely to find the topic of a session particularly sensitive, perhaps due to family circumstances, a disability or a mental health condition. For example, the session Get Moving should be discussed beforehand with children with physical disabilities whose mobility may be limited. This may be done by an adult such as a learning support assistant who is specifically involved in the care of the child, a staff member who has pastoral responsibility such as a form tutor, or a school counsellor. It may be appropriate to allow the child to withdraw from the lesson, and without having to explain their absence to the rest of the class. If it is necessary, it will be important to consider how to follow up the missed lesson with the child in question so that they are able to benefit from the learning. The need for sensitivity to the needs of children who are likely to be at risk during particular sessions has been highlighted in the introductory notes for each session.

Encouraging positive and respectful relationships

Guidance from Section 3 of the PSHE Association's *Education Character Curriculum Planning Toolkit* (2016) emphasises that because PSHE education explores pupils' day-to-day lives, including potentially sensitive and personal issues, it is crucial that teachers establish and maintain a safe teaching and learning environment in the classroom.

A key factor in the success of the programme is that children feel confident enough to express their views and opinions and are able to put what they have learnt into practice in their daily lives. Studies suggest that effective learning is therefore more likely to take place when class teachers as opposed to unfamiliar professionals deliver social and emotional programmes (CASEL 2010; Hattie 2012).

Practitioners have a vital role to play in creating a classroom environment that is characterised by positive and respectful relationships. Positive interactions between adults and children make a significant difference to the emotional climate of the classroom and the school and play a powerful role in reinforcing the key messages of the programme. Relationships are endorsed by what is said and what is not said and the messages that are given about value and expectations. As Clarke (2014, p.23) writes:

> Knowing whether your teacher likes you is a key factor in pupil achievement and confidence as a learner. Children are highly attuned to the subtlest body language, tone of voice or words used by their teachers. We should never forget that children are at the mercy of our attitude towards them, not only as learners, but also as young people.

In a recent newsletter, *Positive Emotions and Purpose in the Classroom*, positive psychologist Robert Brooks (2015) suggests that teachers should appreciate that they have control over a significant dynamic in the classroom, namely the attitudes and behaviours that they choose to adopt and display in the classroom. Teachers, suggests Brooks, can choose to relate to children in a way that conveys the message, 'We care about you and will do our best to help you to learn and to succeed.' This emphasis on respectful relationships recognises that without a safe and positive classroom environment rooted in positive caring relationships, the learning process will be undermined and lead to problems such as a lack of engagement and motivation.

Children who are hard to reach

Children who are hard to reach will, cautions Sue Roffey (2011, p.159), resist all attempts to acknowledge that you care about them:

> This can be for several reasons. The people they really want to care for them are their parents so you are a poor substitute. When a child has been repeatedly let down by others

they will be reluctant to trust an adult. Do not aim to get close to students like this – show them respect and be accepting – but remain at a professional distance.

Creating high-quality connections in the classroom boosts positive feelings, increases the likelihood that children will co-operate and learn from each other, and boosts the energy that children have for persisting at tasks, all of which contribute to a happier and a more productive learning environment. Research conducted at Friedrich Schiller University in Germany (Straube, Sauer and Miltner 2011) suggests that being on the receiving end of a negative commentary can have a harmful effect on your brain, outlook and ability to solve problems. If we mostly tell ourselves negative stories and use more pessimistic explanations, it will undermine our ability to keep going in the face of setbacks, or to look forward with optimism. Jenny Fox-Eades (2008, p.26) explains this very clearly when she writes:

> What is really important about this for teachers is that children mirror the explanatory style of the adults around them. If children hear adults saying *typical this always happens to me, nothing ever works round here, nobody cares* etc then they will start to use these 'stories' for themselves. Such stories, very simply, undermine their ability to learn and to achieve their academic potential.

Building a growth mindset

Central to what we now know about the brain and how it works is the concept of mindsets. It was originally developed by the American psychologist and professor at Stanford University Carol Dweck, and her research seeks to answer the question: Why do some people achieve their potential while equally talented others don't?

Dweck (2006) has demonstrated that we all do much better if we *believe* that our intelligence is malleable and can increase. Regardless of whether, in fact, the purest type of intelligence is malleable or not, we all do much better if we believe that it is.

Growth and fixed mindsets

Dweck distinguishes between a *growth* and a *fixed* mindset. Individuals with a fixed mindset believe that they are born with a certain amount of intelligence that is fixed for the rest of their lives and cannot be altered. Those with a growth mindset believe that they can 'grow' their intelligence and that it can be increased through effort. This belief creates a learning culture where both children and adults have confidence in themselves and believe that they can succeed.

A growth mindset has become a highly accessible concept for the way learners need to think about themselves in order to become successful learners. Central to the concept of a growth mindset is the belief that our brain can be developed like a muscle, changing and growing stronger the more it is used. In her innovative book *Mindset*, Dweck (2006) emphasises the powerful message that throughout life the brain grows fresh cells whenever we are learning new information and skills. It is therefore *never* too late to learn.

The importance of time, effort, practice and input

The route to developing a 'smarter' brain is through sustained practice and effort. A crucial way of ensuring that there is a positive learning culture in the classroom is to talk with children about the nature of intelligence and how we can grow our abilities through practice and effort. A growth mindset learning culture reduces the fear of failure and encourages children to be open and share their errors and see them as learning opportunities. This is because when we make mistakes and are given an opportunity to receive feedback, it is this feedback that moves us on in our learning.

Highly relevant to the Positive Body Image programme is Tough's (2012) observation in his book *How Children Succeed* that children (and all of us) do better when we have a growth mindset and believe that we can improve our intelligence. This belief, explains Tough, also applies to our character strengths. Thus throughout the programme the importance of presenting strengths and healthy habits not as fixed traits but as constantly developing qualities will inspire children to improve these attributes. Tough (2012, p.98) quotes Mike Witter, an English teacher at a Knowledge is Power Program School in New York, who he considers to be hard-wired to believe in the power of the growth mindset:

> If you're going to be a good teacher, you *have* to believe in malleable intelligence and character is equally malleable. If you teach kids to pay attention to character, their character will transform.

Praise

Praise which focuses on achievement and effort is perhaps one of the most significant ways that teachers can build a growth mindset culture in their classrooms. However, praise has to be given with caution and care. Empty praise can be confusing, as children very easily recognise the subtext, which is that they are being praised for nothing very much at all. The conclusion they are likely to draw from empty praise is that nothing very much is expected of them. As I have previously cautioned (MacConville 2008), unwarranted praise undermines children by communicating low expectations. An important implication of Dweck's (2000, 2006) work into mindsets is to ensure that as practitioners we praise children for:

- effort

- persistence

- the effectiveness of the strategies that they use rather than for their ability or their innate talents.

Metacognition

Metacognition is the term used to describe learning about learning. Whereas the growth mindset gives children a positive attitude and confidence, metacognition gives them the tools to be able to talk about and understand their learning. It is not enough, suggests Clarke (2014), to simply talk to children about effort, for example, without making it clear what it *means* to put effort into a task.

The key learning powers that are promoted throughout the programme include:

- Concentrate
- Don't give up
- Be co-operative
- Be curious
- Have a go
- Use your imagination
- Keep improving
- Enjoy learning.

FACILITATING A GROUP AND PRACTICAL TIPS ON IMPLEMENTING THE STRATEGIES USED IN THE PROGRAMME

Classroom talk

In her book *Changing Behaviour in Schools: Promoting Positive Relationships and Wellbeing,* educational psychologist Sue Roffey (2011) describes a study (Jensen and Kostarova-Unkovska 1998) that took place in Denmark in which children were asked to identify the times in school when they thought they really learnt something. Top of their list was 'debate in the classroom', and at the bottom was 'when the teacher talks'. In line with the findings from this study and advice from the PSHE Association (2012) on handling sensitive or controversial issues, the sessions are carefully structured to ensure that there are opportunities throughout for children to learn from each other through conversations that promote learning and for them to discuss issues in pairs and small groups, as well as sharing views with the class.

Talk Partners

Talk Partners and Snowballing are used throughout the programme to ensure that children discuss and plan together in pairs and in small groups in order to co-operatively improve each other's learning. Throughout the programme the term Snowballing refers to Talk Partners joining up with other pairs to form small groups of 4, 6 or even 8 children, depending on the task. The use of Talk Partners throughout the programme means that all children have:

- a designated partner to talk to
- thinking time after a question is asked by the teacher to the whole class, and an opportunity to articulate their thinking to their Talk Partner
- a variety of different children to talk to throughout the programme.

Random pairing

Talk Partners should be chosen randomly at the beginning of each session so that children have the opportunity to work with a variety of their peers over the course of the programme. Random pairing should be carried out quickly at the beginning of each session. Ways to make the pairings include the teacher choosing:

- lollysticks with children's names

- photos of the children

- matching picture cards (for example, a knife and fork) in a pot or bag

- through a computer randomiser such as *The Hat* from www.harmonyhollow.net.

Clearly measures will need to be in place to avoid the same children being paired too often.

Apart from the appreciated fairness, the social and learning impact of Talk Partners is significant. Children learn the vital life skills of negotiation and co-operation skills, and other benefits of random pairing include the following:

- taking children out of their comfort zone

- challenging them to work on their weaknesses

- shy children have to talk

- talkative children have to listen

- if children are paired with a lower achiever, children often become *explainers*, a higher-order skill which deepens their learning

- children are paired with a higher achiever and have opportunities to learn.

Answering whole-class questions

Randomly selecting who will answer a class question through, for example, the use of named lollysticks creates an inclusive learning culture and avoids what is sometimes referred to as the damaging 'hands-up culture' where not enough 'wait time' is given to children, especially those with learning or social and emotional needs, to answer questions. Studies suggest that in traditional classrooms the same children tend to be the first with their hands up, thus distracting and detracting from other children's thinking.

Talk Partners allows children time to think after a question is asked to the whole class and is also an opportunity to express their thoughts, for example you have 30 seconds to talk to your Talk Partner about that question. Once children have had an opportunity to discuss their thinking with their Talk Partner, anyone should then be able to answer a question that has been put to the whole class. This also has the desired effect of keeping all children focused and alert in case they are called on to answer the question. However, randomly choosing children to answer a question asked to the whole class without first giving them an opportunity to discuss it with their Talk Partner is not productive and can reinforce a fixed mindset. Clarke (2014) suggests that it is the articulation of the thinking, and being privileged enough to hear someone else's ideas, that enables children to be able to confidently answer questions at random.

Group work

Two pairs of Talk Partners can join up or 'snowball' to make a group of four children. The ability to work in different groups is fundamental to social and emotional learning. Group work involves four or more children working together on a common group activity with shared goals that require them to:

- each contribute to the task

- help each other by using appropriate social skills such as active listening and turn taking

- ask relevant questions

- provide helpful responses

- promote each other's learning.

During teacher-led activities, breaking up a lesson with opportunities for group activities can clarify new learning, enable children to share ideas, increase their understanding, and add further meaning to the content of the session. Structured group work also promotes understanding and social and emotional learning, and increases a sense of belonging and connection to the school.

Answering children's questions

As the programme is about the children themselves and their day-to-day experiences, it is likely that they are going to be engaged in the topics that are introduced throughout the programme and seek further information. The PSHE Association (2013) provides helpful advice for teachers on answering children's questions. The key skill involved is recognising the *type* of question being asked in order to be able to respond appropriately. The following examples of the types of questions that children may ask provide a helpful guide.

It may be a question that:

- demonstrates that the pupil does not understand

- is seeking clarification

- shows the pupil knows the answer but wants reassurance

- can be answered and is of interest to the whole class

- requires an individual response later

- is designed to make the class laugh

- is designed to elicit personal information from the teacher.

The PSHE guidance suggests that perhaps, most importantly, it will be reassuring for practitioners to know that not all questions require an immediate answer. The following 'holding' response is suggested:

That is a really interesting question and I need a little time to give you a really good answer.

This both respects the pupil's curiosity and gives the teacher time to devise an appropriate answer. Teachers should feel confident about giving themselves some thinking time, or time to consult with a colleague or check a school policy, before answering.

SUPPORTING DIFFERENT LEARNING NEEDS

The following strategies are used throughout the programme to ensure that the learning environment is inclusive of *all* learners:

- Pre-teaching sessions: the provision of a short pre-teaching session for children with special educational needs, particularly those with speech and language or learning difficulties, means they can be taught the key vocabulary that will be used in the session.

- Talk Partners: the use of Talk Partners throughout the programme means that *all* children are fully included in the sessions and all have the same opportunities to discuss their learning with a peer and co-operatively improve each other's learning together.

- Talk Partners allows *all* children time to think after a question is asked and gives them an opportunity to put their thinking into words. This strategy is particularly relevant for children with social and communication difficulties (for example, those with Asperger syndrome or autism spectrum disorder) who would otherwise be at risk of social isolation in a mainstream learning environment.

- Working with a Talk Partner also means that shy children, those with speech and language difficulties and those with sensory impairment can have their first breakthroughs of speaking out in class.

- Talk Partners enhances social inclusion, as random pairing avoids the inevitability of children being left out and never chosen as a partner, or children not wanting to talk to certain children if they are simply asked to turn to the person next to them.

- Talk Partners also benefits low achievers who may not be confident to express their ideas to the whole class but are willing to do so to a partner or in a small group.

- Random pairing promotes peer collaboration, which is important, especially to those children with low self-esteem or who lack social confidence and expect not to be chosen by a peer.

- The use of drawings, cartoons and Mind Maps is encouraged throughout the programme to ensure that children with literacy difficulties (for example, specific learning difficulties, like dyslexia) are not excluded from the process of completing tasks and developing their programme log. Encouraging *all* children to express themselves creatively and in a variety of ways is vital to the success, creativity and enjoyment of the programme. Additionally, an available adult to scribe children's views or help with spellings may be required in some classrooms.

- Adult assistance may be necessary to encourage children with low self-esteem who may be reluctant to participate in the sessions which focus on children exploring their strengths and talents.

- Extension activities are provided throughout the programme to provide further learning opportunities for those children who are keen to extend their learning about a topic and for those children who are recognised to be high achievers.

Specific arrangements for children with disabilities

In addition to the inclusive strategies described above, there are also a number of specific arrangements that may need to be put in place for children with low-incident sensory disabilities. These children may need to be given preferential seating towards the front of the class. Children with visual impairment may require the print size of the activity sheets to be enlarged or, in very rare cases, to be reduced.

It will be important to check with the SENCO (special educational needs co-ordinator) or inclusion manager the specific classroom arrangements that may need to be in place for individual children with disabilities and the specialist equipment that individual children may require in order to access the sessions. It will be for the teacher to check whether individual children should be wearing hearing aids or glasses and also whether they require classroom equipment such as magnifiers, close circuit televisions or radio aids to be in place.

Recommended reading and a list of useful websites for supporting different learning needs can be found at the end of this book.

CHAPTER 4

STAFF TRAINING

This chapter contains a presentation of 16 slides with additional notes and activities to support the facilitator in delivering the programme. The purpose of the presentation is to, first, introduce participants to the concepts and issues surrounding positive body image and, second, to provide a practical guide to delivering the programme.

Body image is an area of increasing concern for children and young people, parents and teachers. Studies suggest that primary schools can play a significant role in enabling children to develop a positive body image. Although traditionally this domain has been viewed as the task of secondary schools, children at an increasingly young age report being besieged by unrealistic images of beauty, which leads to a lack of confidence and low self-esteem. The *Reflections on Body Image* report (APPG 2012) suggests that girls as young as five years of age are already aware of diet practices and the cultural pressure to be thin. A review of programmes by McCabe, Ricciardelli and Holt (2005) suggests that interventions that target younger children and are designed to increase their resilience and promote a healthy sense of self-worth are more effective because beliefs become more entrenched in adolescence.

The aim of the training session is to:

- raise awareness about the importance of addressing positive body image

- prompt reflection, discussion and practical action around how to develop a body-image-friendly environment for all children, regardless of body shape, ethnicity and other physical features such as disability

- establish an approach to promoting positive body image through building self-esteem, resilience and healthy living skills.

The training session has been designed to enable teachers to approach the delivery of the programme in their classrooms with confidence. It addresses the range of issues that are likely to arise in teaching this sensitive subject, provides an opportunity for teachers to prepare for tasks, and addresses their concerns with colleagues prior to delivering the programme.

The Positive Body Image programme takes a strengths-based approach. This means that, throughout the programme, the character strengths and capabilities of children are emphasised. Positive psychologists agree that enabling children to identify their strengths is what enables them to build their resilience, manage uncertain times and deal with media pressures that put children at risk for developing body dissatisfaction.

In preparation for the session and to familiarise themselves with the 24 character strengths that underpin the programme, teachers may wish to take 20 minutes to discover their VIA (Values in Action) character strengths at www.authentichappiness.com.

THE WORKSHOP

Resources required for delivering the training:

- Positive Body Image programme: list of sessions

- Useful resources.

SLIDE 1

POSITIVE BODY IMAGE FOR KIDS:
A STRENGTHS-BASED CURRICULUM FOR CHILDREN AGED 7–11

Facilitator's notes

The aim of this presentation is twofold. First, it will introduce practitioners to the main issues surrounding the concept of body image. Second, it will outline the contents of the programme and provide practitioners with a guide to its delivery.

Available at www.jkp.com/voucher using the code MACCONVILLEPOSITIVE

SLIDE 2

What is body image?

The term 'body image' refers to our idea of how our body looks, how we feel about our appearance and how attractive we perceive ourselves to be to others. This mental picture of how we think we look and how we appear to others is independent of our actual appearance.

Our body image changes in response to feedback from others. Our friends, peers, family, lifestyle, cultural background and the media can all influence our body image.

Anyone, whatever they look like, can have a positive or negative body image.

The term 'body image' was first coined by Paul Ferdinand Schilder (1886–1940), an Austrian psychiatrist and psychoanalyst and student of Sigmund Freud, when he used it in his book *The Image and Appearance of the Human Body*, which was published in 1937.

Facilitator's notes

Body image is the picture we hold in our mind about our physical appearance. It includes how we feel about the size, shape, weight and appearance of our bodies. The term 'body image' is not new. Although it was first used as a medical and psychological term, today the term is in widespread use.

Our body image can be positive or negative. Negative body issues or 'body dissatisfaction' may not be consistent with how we look in reality. Marilyn Monroe, for example, who was noted for her outstanding beauty, in fact felt that she had many body defects.

Negative body image can range from those individuals who are only moderately dissatisfied with their appearance, through those who are suffering body image disturbance as a result of an injury, wound, disfigurement or disability, to those who are suffering from eating disorders or extreme body dissatisfaction, i.e. body dysmorphic disorder (BDD).

Activity

Provide an opportunity for participants to ask questions and seek clarification of the term 'body image'.

The term 'body image' originated as a medical and psychological term. Ask participants to discuss whether they consider that is how it is viewed today.

Available at www.jkp.com/voucher using the code MACCONVILLEPOSITIVE

SLIDE 3

Our self-esteem and body image are inextricably linked and form the fabric of how we think about ourselves.

Having a positive body image and feeling comfortable about the way we look is an essential part of our self-esteem and our overall emotional health and well-being.

Body dissatisfaction, however, can have a very pervasive effect on our well-being. It can undermine our capacity to enjoy life, prevent us enjoying positive relationships with others, and stop us taking on new challenges and experiences. Body dissatisfaction can also cause anxiety and lead to depression.

Facilitator's notes

Having a positive body image and feeling confident about our appearance improves our outlook, provides us with social confidence, and gives us the freedom to approach new challenges and experiences with confidence.

Because our feelings about how we look are so inextricably linked to our overall view of ourselves, being dissatisfied with our appearance results in low self-esteem. Body dissatisfaction can also lead to low mood, depression, anxiety and, in extreme cases, to obsessive over-exercising, strict dieting and a reluctance to socialise or even engage with others.

Activity

Provide participants with an opportunity to discuss the importance of having a positive body image and to suggest why body dissatisfaction is increasingly widespread among children and young people.

Ask participants to consider the relevance of these issues to their work in schools and, if possible, to think about them in the context of a young person they currently work with.

Take feedback.

SLIDE 4

For very young children body image is a natural fact of life. Young children do not usually judge or evaluate each other's appearance; they accept each other as they are. Placing a value on how we look ourselves and how others look is something that gradually happens throughout childhood for the following reasons:

- events that draw attention to our body, for example illness, trauma, puberty

- parental criticism/teasing about our appearance

- our preferences, for example straight hair to curly hair, blue eyes to brown eyes

- exposure to media messages with their unrealistic imagery, airbrushing and size zero models.

(Kater 2004)

Facilitator's notes

Children's body image develops based on the interactions with the people and the world around them. Young children do not need outside cues and prompts to tell them what they feel. This is because they are securely connected to their inner experiences. Reinforcing body esteem in young children means helping them to stay connected to and maintain trust in themselves and in the truth of their own experiences.

As they grow and develop, children are increasingly subject to messages that contradict what they know to be true. Fat children are often told that they can't be hungry; attractive children are told that they can't be lonely. If messages regularly contradict what children know to be true, trust in who they are and therefore their body esteem begins to break down. From an early age it is important to reinforce children's healthy body esteem so that they are less likely to disconnect from what they really need for health and well-being. Help children to maintain positive self-esteem and understand how to effectively challenge the pervasive messages that support negative body image attitudes and unhealthy eating.

Activity

Ask participants to discuss with a partner or in a small group the view that it takes active adult participation to enable children as they grow to maintain positive self-esteem. Take feedback from this discussion and record their responses.

Available at www.jkp.com/voucher using the code MACCONVILLEPOSITIVE

SLIDE 5

As they get older, children's body image usually begins to take on increasing significance and they begin to recognise that how they look may be evaluated positively or negatively. These feelings increasingly involve a sense of vulnerability. Kater (2004) suggests that how much vulnerability depends on:

- a child's sensitivity to criticism

- personality type

- the extent to which the child's appearance fits the 'cultural ideal'

- the nature, frequency and intensity of media messages that the child is exposed to.

Facilitator's notes

Messages about the looks to have and the *right* appearance are delivered to children every day, without a warning that tells them these messages are untrue and can undermine their health and quality of life. These messages come not only from television, radio and magazines – they pop up on computer screens, slide by on the side of buses, and stare out from larger-than-life photos in shop windows. It is impossible to escape them. It is not explained to children that nearly all these messages exist to undermine their confidence and to make money for someone. The more vulnerable a child is, the more that child will be influenced by these media messages.

Activity

Ask participants if they agree, based on their practical experience in schools, with the list of the factors that can contribute to children's feelings of vulnerability about their appearance. Are there any other factors they would add to the list?

Ask participants to explore with a partner or in a small group their own experience of children they have worked with and how any of the factors that can contribute to children's feelings of vulnerability have affected them about how they look.

Take feedback from this discussion and ask for practical suggestions of what can be done to reduce any feelings of vulnerability children may experience in school because of their appearance.

SLIDE 6

The All Party Parliamentary Group (APPG) on Body Image was formed in 2011 in response to growing concern about the negative effects of body dissatisfaction on national well-being.

The inquiry found that negative body image is a:

- cause of health and relationship problems

- contributor to low self-esteem

- major barrier to participation in school.

Its subsequent report, *Reflections on Body Image* (APPG 2012), outlined the key findings of the inquiry and proposed recommendations to tackle increasing levels of unhealthy eating behaviours and body image dissatisfaction especially among children and young people.

Facilitator's notes

The *Reflections on Body Image* report concluded that body dissatisfaction is on the increase and is now one of the biggest causes of anxiety for an increasing number of children, both boys and girls. Although historically body image dissatisfaction is something that has been associated with adolescent girls, the inquiry found that:

- boys are increasingly affected by body dissatisfaction

- girls as young as five years of age are worried about the way they look because they have begun to recognise that certain body types are more acceptable than others

- many young girls diet and boys over-exercise to achieve society's view of the *ideal* body.

Activity

Ask participants for their comments on these findings.

Ask participants whether, based on their experience of the children and young people they work with, they are aware of the reported increasing levels of body dissatisfaction.

Take feedback.

Available at www.jkp.com/voucher using the code MACCONVILLEPOSITIVE

SLIDE 7

The *Reflections on Body Image* report (APPG 2012) emphasised the need to equip children and young people with robust tools with which to challenge unrealistic beauty ideals and successfully handle media pressure so that they are able to resist its negative influences.

Recommendations included the following:

- provide role models who are able to affirm children's self-worth in other ways, rather than through their appearance

- teach media literacy skills and enable children to question and challenge the unrealistic or unhealthy media messages that promote the thin ideal

- enable children to maintain and celebrate their innate body esteem.

Facilitator's notes

The All Party Parliamentary Group report *Reflections on Body Image* recommended that although children are born with confidence in their bodies, an increasing number of girls and boys succumb to the media pressures that convince them that how they look is more important than who they are. It is not only media messages that influence children – they also learn the value of the 'right' appearance when familiar adults in their day-to-day lives greet each other with comments such as 'You look great! Have you lost weight?' Children learn unintentional lessons about appearance when they hear adults expressing dissatisfaction with their bodies. It is important, therefore, that we are aware that we are important role models for children. As the APPG report (2012, p.16) emphasised, 'Children are affected by the people closest to them – so what the peergroup says, what their parents say and what teachers say is going to be incredibly important.'

It is also important that we encourage children to question the media messages that convey the importance of conforming to the 'right' appearance, and we should point out that these messages exist to make money for companies.

Activity

Ask participants whether they agree with these recommendations. Are there any further recommendations that they would make? What do they consider are practical steps that they could take in the school to enable young children to maintain their positive body image?

Take feedback.

SLIDE 8

The key characteristics of positive body image:

- Valuing your body for what it can do

- Accepting and loving your body

- Having a sense of optimism and a positive outlook on life

- Appreciating different types of beauty

- Challenging media messages that promote the ultra-thin ideal

- Knowing that you are loved and accepted by important others

- Choosing friends who have a healthy attitude to their appearance

- Taking care of your body by eating healthily, taking regular exercise and getting enough rest.

Facilitator's notes

The *Reflections on Body Image* report (APPG 2012) also emphasised the importance of encouraging children to recognise and value their innate body esteem. However, in order to do this it is important to recognise what these characteristics are. The key characteristics of positive body image describe features that are wide ranging and show that self-esteem and body image are inextricably linked. Body image encompasses what we think of our physical bodies, while self-esteem encompasses feelings about our worth as individuals. The two are woven together to form the fabric of how we feel about ourselves. Individuals with healthy self-esteem generally feel positive about their appearance; and feeling good about our body, our appearance, our strengths and our capabilities enhances our self-esteem.

Activity

Ask participants to read the list of the characteristics of a healthy body image and discuss them with a partner or in a small group. Provide an opportunity for participants to ask questions and seek clarification on these characteristics. Ask participants if there are any other characteristics that they would add to this list.

Take feedback.

SLIDE 9

The key factors that promote positive body image:

- A strong sense of belonging and feeling loved by family and friends

- A supportive environment that accepts many different types of beauty

- Being media literate and not taking media messages at face value.

Facilitator's notes

Parents, particularly, have a considerable influence on the relationship between appearance and self-esteem in their children. Although parents generally report that they like the way their child looks in younger childhood, this can change as children get older. Parents can influence their children by conveying their own appearance-related anxieties and behaviours or through their attitude to the appearance of their child. Children from families who buy into society's value of the importance of appearance above all else are most at risk for body dissatisfaction and a negative self-image.

However, parents who believe that it is what's on the inside of a person that counts and not their appearance, and who accept people for what they are, not for what they look like, recognising that people come in all shapes and sizes, can help to ensure that their child has a positive body image.

Mass media, including television, magazines and advertisements, tends to promote a rigid and narrow ideal of attractiveness. Magazines targeted at pre-teens and adolescent girls contain numerous articles on how to 'improve' their appearance, for example through dieting, exercise and makeovers. Media literacy refers to children's ability to identify and analyse different types of media messages and photoshopped advertisements and become skilled at decoding and recognising what's really going on behind these messages.

If harmful media influences are a risk factor for developing body dissatisfaction, media literacy techniques to reduce or eliminate the power of negative media messages should reduce their impact. Media literacy or the ability to decode media messages and their intent helps to decrease children's vulnerability to the media.

Activity

Provide an opportunity for participants to discuss these key factors and suggest any additional factors that they consider may contribute to body dissatisfaction in children and young people.

Available at www.jkp.com/voucher using the code MACCONVILLEPOSITIVE

SLIDE 10
POSITIVE BODY IMAGE FOR KIDS:
A STRENGTHS-BASED CURRICULUM FOR CHILDREN AGED 7–11

Facilitator's notes

The aim of the programme is to enable children to maintain and celebrate their innate healthy body esteem and explore the basic building blocks of healthy living. It is also about enabling children to recognise and own their strengths and talents and develop the resilience that will enable them to respond positively to adversity and challenge.

The programme consists of 16 sessions, which explore the basic building blocks of building strengths and healthy living. The sessions are designed to be interactive, with an emphasis on discussion, group and partner work.

SLIDE 11

The sessions:

1. Introduction
2. Bounce back muscles
3. Strengths spotting
4. Here and now
5. The real you
6. Healthy eating habits: three to remember
7. Get moving
8. Have fun
9. Television turnoff
10. Think twice
11. Pictures, pictures everywhere!
12. Thought catching
13. My ABC
14. How to be a friend
15. My hero
16. WOOP

Facilitator's notes

The sessions that form the programme are listed above in the order in which they are presented. They have been selected on the basis that they are recognised to be the key skills associated with maintaining and celebrating a healthy body image, strengthening resilience and building healthy living skills.

Distribute a copy of one of the sessions to the participants and discuss its format with the group in order to increase their familiarity with the programme and their confidence in delivering the sessions.

Activity

Provide an opportunity for participants to seek clarification on the practical aspects of delivering the programme.

Available at www.jkp.com/voucher using the code MACCONVILLEPOSITIVE

SLIDE 12
SLIDE A
A STRENGTHS-BASED APPROACH

A strengths-based approach focuses on the development of capabilities and competencies within both children and adults to help them to solve problems and live their lives in a more effective manner. A strengths-based approach is not so much a series of techniques as a personal perspective that can have a significant impact on how individuals process life events and how they view themselves.

Facilitator's notes

Positive psychologists agree that using our strengths increases our well-being and resilience and makes us more successful at what we do. Strengths are durable, fundamental qualities that describe us at our best. They are qualities like courage, kindness, persistence, curiosity and love. There is a growing awareness that the weakness or deficit correction model of growth is less effective than seeking to identify and build on strengths. The real potential for growth, development and success lies in your existing areas of strengths.

Strengths are important because they become part of each individual's personal identity. They enable children to discover and use their personal power positively and productively. Children who do not discover their strengths can become anxious and uncertain or frustrated and aimless. Every child needs to find their dynamic power and be supported to build their strengths so that they can be successful.

The bottom line of a strengths-based approach is that a child with a strong identity and a stable, positive sense of self and belonging will be far less likely to succumb to the media pressures and commercialism which increasingly feature in every child's world.

Character strengths

In the context of positive psychology, 'strengths' refers to the 24 qualities that were identified by Martin Seligman, the architect of positive psychology, and Chris Peterson. These qualities were selected, following extensive research, on the basis that they are universally respected and valued in every society and era. The list includes traditional traits like bravery, citizenship, fairness, wisdom and integrity; others are concerned with emotions such as love, humour, zest and appreciation of beauty; and some are more concerned with day-to-day interactions, like social intelligence, kindness and gratitude. According to Peterson and Seligman (2004), these strengths can be developed and they underpin good character formation – hence they are frequently referred to as 'character strengths'. Their value comes from their practical benefits – what you gain by possessing and expressing them. Cultivating these strengths represents a reliable path to the good life, a life that is not just happy but also meaningful and fulfilling.

The strengths-based approach that underpins the Positive Body Image programme includes an emphasis on the character strengths that were identified by Peterson and Seligman. It also encompasses practical skills and talents and the learning powers that are associated with metacognition.

SLIDE 13

Active learning strategies

Children are more likely to build healthy living skills when:

- they learn about these behaviours through enjoyable participatory activities rather than when they are simply given the facts

- sessions emphasise a 'strengths-based approach', i.e. the positive, appealing aspects of healthy living (rather than the negative consequences)

- these benefits are explained in the context of what is already important and relevant to children

- children are encouraged to engage in healthy living habits and behaviours throughout the programme and to continue to use them in their everyday lives.

Facilitator's notes

When delivering the programme it is important that you use approaches that are interactive and engage all learners. This can be achieved by using demonstration, discussion and partner work.

Active participation in the programme will enable children to develop the attitudes and skills that they need to make healthy choices in their day-to-day lives.

Activity

Provide an opportunity for participants to ask questions and seek clarification on the content, structure and practical aspects of delivering the programme.

SLIDE 14

Teaching sensitive issues

When teaching topics which are about the children themselves it is important to:

- understand what prior learning the children are bringing to the classroom

- always establish a safe classroom environment by involving children in setting clear ground rules and reviewing them at the beginning of every session

- consider how you will support a child who you believe to be at risk prior to the session

- consider how you will deal with a child who becomes distressed during the session

- explore the use of techniques to distance the children from the issues that will be raised in the sessions, such as using stories, film clips and photos, or asking the children to imagine how somebody else would feel in the situation.

Facilitator's notes

Discuss with the group the issues listed above. Emphasise that because of the nature of the programme some sensitive issues may be brought up or individual children may become upset during the session. It is crucial, therefore, that lesson preparation and delivery is sensitive to differing needs and perspectives and to bear in mind that there may be some children in the class who are particularly vulnerable. These may include children with special educational needs and disabilities, those on the Child Protection Register, or children in local authority care. There may also be children who are overweight or who suffer from eating disorders.

As the programme takes a strengths-based approach and emphasises the capabilities, character strengths and talents of each individual, it will be appropriate to meet the social and emotional needs of each child. Also, the use of inclusive strategies such as Talk Partners and Circle Time that are used throughout the programme will mean that each child will be fully included in classroom discussions.

If a child does become upset during a session, offer them support and encouragement and make time to speak to them after the session. It may be necessary in some cases to refer the child in question to the school counsellor. If in doubt regarding next steps, take advice from your line manager or the school's safeguarding officer. It will be important for facilitators to be aware of the school's policies on safeguarding, confidentiality and child protection.

A confidential letter box placed in the classroom throughout the programme will provide all children with the opportunity to write down anything that is worrying them and post it in the letter box so that it can be dealt with privately with the child.

Ensure that the children are aware of the confidential sources of support that are available to them, for example access to ChildLine and, if necessary, with parental permission, to other sources of support such as the school counsellor and a Circle of Friends intervention.

Activity

Ask the participants to explore the issues listed above in pairs or small groups. Take feedback on the discussion, identifying clear points of action for each one.

Available at www.jkp.com/voucher using the code MACCONVILLEPOSITIVE

SLIDE 15

Facilitator's notes

Celebrating is a provocative act. It is about focusing on what is good in life and what has gone well, and building shared and happy memories.

Positive psychology teaches us that we get more of what we focus on, so if we celebrate regularly we will find even more to celebrate. Celebration builds relationships, improves our mood and helps us to feel positive about ourselves and others. The final session in the programme:

- celebrates the learning and the working together that has taken place throughout the programme

- acknowleges children individually by name for their hard work and contribution to the programme and awards each child with a certificate

- emphasises a sense of hopefulness and looking to the future in the goal-setting activity WOOP

- celebrates a positive end to the programme by providing a party for children.

Positive psychologists put a particular emphasis on positive endings because studies suggest that our emotional memories depend on how an experience ends. Children's parties, for example, usually conclude with a goody bag. Thus practitioners invariably ensure that lessons, mentoring sessions, the school day, the end of terms and the academic year end on a positive and celebratory note. It is important to conclude activities and events with a focus on positive moments and what has gone well. Consciously ending on a high note is called the 'peak end rule' and is what will help to make any 'lows' disappear when we look back on an event.

Activity

Celebrating is a habit that can significantly increase our well-being. Ask participants to explore with a partner how they can build the 'peak end rule' and the habit of celebrating into their work.

Conclude the session by asking participants to share with a partner what went well for them during the session.

Take feedback.

SLIDE 16

Further information

- Useful websites
- Recommended reading
- Helpful organisations.

Facilitator's notes

Highlight any resources you have compiled (from the Further Information section at the back of the book) that may be of particular value to the group.

Thank participants for attending the session and wish them success in delivering the programme.

CHAPTER 5

THE SESSIONS

SESSION 1: INTRODUCTION TO THE POSITIVE BODY IMAGE PROGRAMME

Learning objectives

We are learning to:

- understand what a 'body image' is

- agree our class rules so that we can learn safely together.

Learning outcomes

I can:

- describe what a 'body image' is

- tell you the rules that we have agreed for our class

- explain how our rules can help us work together.

Resources

Activity for Class discussion:

- Healthy habits build a positive body image

Right Now activity:

- Our class rules

Take Away activity:

- How to be an amazing Talk Partner

Key vocabulary

- body image

- believe

- appearance

- rules

- positive

- negative

- celebrate

Pre-teaching session

Children with special educational needs and disabilities may benefit from a short pre-teaching session to introduce them to the key vocabulary that is used in this session. (For guidance on differentiation see page 62.)

Introduction (approx. 10 mins)

Write the words *body image* on the board and ask the class to suggest what it means. Scribe the responses.

Starter activity: Draw and Write: What is a positive body image? (approx. 10 mins)

Ask each child to respond to this statement by drawing a picture and using words and/or writing notes to explain it. (For guidance on Draw and Write activities see page 41.) It is important to be aware that, for a variety of reasons, some children may suffer from concerns/ worries about their appearance. An additional adult may therefore need to be available to assist them with this activity and provide reassurance and encouragement.

Class discussion (approx. 10 mins)

Explain that our body image is what we *think* and how we *feel* about our appearance. It is not about how we actually look in real life but what we *believe* and how we *feel* about our appearance. Anyone, whatever they look like, can have a positive body image, or they can feel unhappy about how they look and have a negative body image. This means that two people who look very similar may both feel very differently about how they look. Ask for suggestions about why somebody (not themselves) might have a positive or a negative body image. (For guidance on using distancing techniques to enable children to avoid personalising issues see page 51.)

If the class is reluctant to share ideas, the following questions may be used to promote discussion:

- What messages might a person have heard about how they look?

- What experiences might they have had?

- What might they say to themselves that makes them feel happy or unhappy with how they look?

Scribe responses in two columns under the headings:

- Positive body image

- Negative body image.

Ask for suggestions of what advice they would give to somebody who was unhappy with their appearance to help them feel better about themselves. Explain that during the programme we are going to be learning about all the different things that can help us build and celebrate our positive body image. Ask the class for suggestions of what these might be and record their responses.

If the class is reluctant to make suggestions, ask them to score themselves on the activity sheet *Healthy habits build a positive body image.*

Share and explain the learning objective and learning outcome with the class:

- We are learning to understand what a body image is

- I can tell you what a positive body image is.

Discuss with the class that when we are learning about a positive body image it is important that we have some rules to help everybody feel safe and work well together. (Note: The aim of this discussion is to ensure that children are aware that rules are not just restrictions but can enable them to feel safe and know that things are fair.)

Ask the class for suggestions of what rules would help them all when they are working together. Record their responses.

Suggest that talking to each other in pairs or small groups rather than always talking together as a whole class means that everybody gets more time to talk. Talking can help our thinking and can also give everyone in the class an opportunity to share their ideas.

Talk Partners

Explain to the class that for the purposes of the programme each child will have a Talk Partner for each session. Explain that the Talk Partners will be chosen fairly using *random pairings*. Explain to the class what system will be used to make the pairings. Allocate each child in the class a Talk Partner. (For guidance on using Talk Partners and making random pairings see page 60.)

Right Now activity: Our class rules (approx. 15 mins)

Distribute a copy of *Our class rules* to each child. Ask the children to sit with their Talk Partners and read out each rule in turn and together agree about the following:

- a helpful rule for classroom talk (colour the box green)

- not a helpful rule (colour the box red)

- not sure if it is a helpful rule or not (colour the box orange).

They should then add two further rules that they think would be helpful.

Mid-session learning stop (approx. 5 mins)

Step 1

Randomly choose a child so that the whole class is focused as nobody knows who will be selected. Ask the child to:

- explain where they are up to with completing the task

- read out the rules that they have agreed are helpful, the rules that are not helpful, the rules that they are unsure about and any new rules they have added

- explain how they went about making these decisions.

Step 2

Ask the rest of the class to reflect on their work in a similar way. Allow time for the class to complete the activity and then *snowball*, i.e. join up with two other Talk Partners to make a group of six children. Each group should then complete a joint *Our class rules* by sharing and building on the original choices that the class made with their Talk Partner.

Ask the groups to decide who will report back to the class, and allow time for the groups to complete the task (approx. 5 mins).

Class discussion (approx. 10 mins)

Ask each group to report back on the rules that they agreed on. Complete a tally chart so that the children can see which rules get the most votes. Decide on a set of approximately six rules and, if possible, incorporate some of the rules that were generated by the class.

Take Away activity: How to be an amazing Talk Partner

- Distribute the Take Away activity to the class.

- Ask the children to think about how well they worked with their Talk Partner and in the group; who made a good suggestion, listened carefully to others, took turns, had good ideas? Suggest that the class uses similar ideas to complete the activity.

Final plenary: reflect and review (approx. 10 mins)

- Revisit the learning objectives and outcomes for the session and, with the class, discuss whether they have been met.

- Encourage the class to ask any questions that they have in relation to the session. Children who are able to communicate in writing can be encouraged to submit anonymous questions after the session by using the question box.

- With their Talk Partner, ask the children to talk through and then individually, using a different colour pen, add any new learning and ideas to the Draw and Write activity *What is a positive body image?* from the beginning of the session.

- End the session with *Pass the smile* or a similar closure activity. (For guidance on closure activities see page 44.)

After the session:

- make a poster of *Our class rules* and display it in the classroom

- provide copies for each child to sign and store in their programme log.

Note: The class rules should be reviewed at the beginning of each subsequent session and referred to when necessary throughout the sessions to ensure that there is a safe and productive environment for all learners.

Name: _____ Date: _____

HEALTHY HABITS BUILD A POSITIVE BODY IMAGE

A = always, B = sometimes, C = never

Score your healthy habits and put A, B or C in the boxes below to show the strategies used.

I have a good breakfast ☐	I drink lots of water ☐	I phone my friends ☐
I play sports ☐	I take a dog for a walk ☐	I manage my time well ☐
I go to bed at a reasonable time ☐	I get enough sleep ☐	I have a hobby I enjoy ☐
I go for a daily jog ☐	I look for the positives ☐	I have friends who care about me ☐
I watch TV ☐	I eat chocolate ☐	I enjoy a mix of foods ☐
I am happy to see my friends ☐	I enjoy listening to friends' good news ☐	I talk to parents ☐
I talk to another adult ☐	I don't go on first impressions ☐	I look on the bright side ☐
I build happy memories ☐	I listen to music ☐	

Count your As, Bs and Cs. My score is: A: _____   B: _____   C: _____

I rate my life as: healthy, quite healthy, not healthy at all.

These habits would help me to be more healthy:

1. _____

2. _____

3. _____

Copyright © Ruth MacConville 2017

OUR CLASS RULES

Names:

Talk together and COLOUR:

    GREEN – good ideas

    RED – not good ideas

    ORANGE – not sure

Talk together and DECIDE:

- Choose four green ideas.
  We choose numbers:

  ☐ ☐ ☐ ☐

- Make up two good ideas of your own.
  Write them in the circles.

1. We will take turns to talk and listen

2. We will try to reach a shared agreement

3. Everyone must do what the leader says

4. No one can change their mind

5. Everyone will talk as loudly as they can

6. We will co-operate – try to get along with each other

7. We will listen to and think about each other's ideas

8. Ask for reasons

9. We think it's best to share our thoughts

Copyright © Ruth MacConville 2017

HOW TO BE AN AMAZING TALK PARTNER

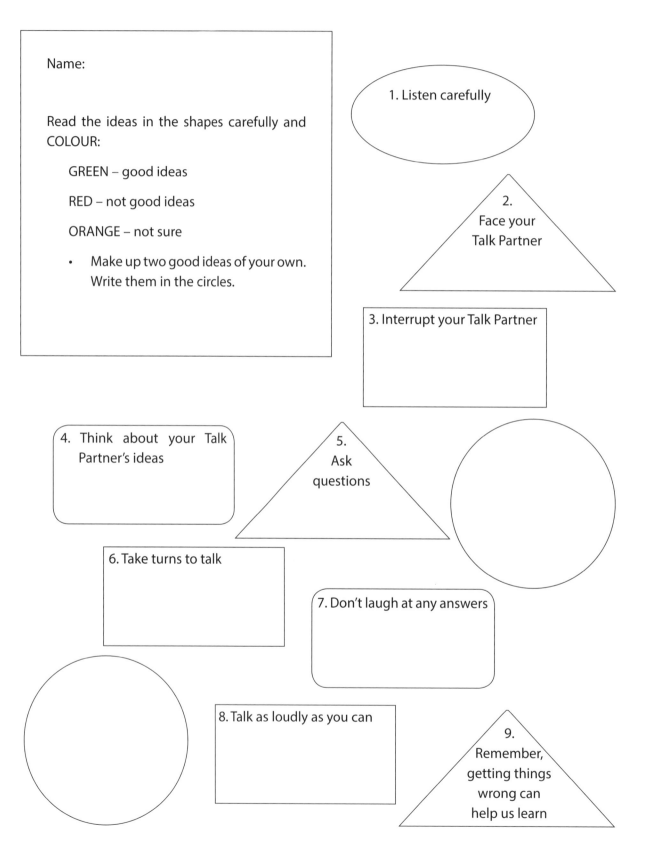

Name:

Read the ideas in the shapes carefully and COLOUR:

GREEN – good ideas

RED – not good ideas

ORANGE – not sure

- Make up two good ideas of your own. Write them in the circles.

1. Listen carefully

2. Face your Talk Partner

3. Interrupt your Talk Partner

4. Think about your Talk Partner's ideas

5. Ask questions

6. Take turns to talk

7. Don't laugh at any answers

8. Talk as loudly as you can

9. Remember, getting things wrong can help us learn

Copyright © Ruth MacConville 2017

SESSION 2: BUILD YOUR BOUNCE BACK MUSCLES

Background notes

The key message of this session is that resilient individuals with a positive body image feel good about themselves, and when they get into tricky situations or feel challenged can draw on the protective factors, i.e. their personal strengths and the people that they can rely on to help them. Resilience is a learned skill. This means that building our resilience is like building up muscles in the gym. If we use and exercise them they become strong. For the purposes of this programme, an individual's personal strengths are called *bounce back muscles*. Edith H. Grotberg (1995), a world-renowned educational psychologist, states that resilient children with healthy self-esteem draw from three main sources of personal strength: *I have, I am, I can*. A fourth bounce back muscle, *I like*, introduced by Boniwell and Ryan (2012), has been added to Grotberg's original list.

The resilient child with a positive body image is one who can say:

- I can (my skills, abilities, talents)

- I have (my family, friends)

- I am (my personal qualities, talents and strengths)

- I like (my hobbies, interests and the things that I enjoy doing)

(Adapted from Grotberg 1995)

According to Grotberg, to be resilient a child needs to have at least two of these personal strengths. If a child has healthy self-esteem (I am), for example, but lacks anyone that they can turn to for support (I have), and does not have the capacity to solve problems (I can), they will not be resilient. This finding is in line with other studies (Brooks and Goldstein 2013; Masten 2014) that show that resilience is the product of a number of mutually enhancing protective factors.

The quiz that children complete during the session calculates their bounce back muscles scores. In addition to drawing children's attention to their areas of strengths, the results of this short quiz can also alert teachers to children who may have low scores in one or more of its sections, signalling that they may require focused intervention to address a possible need.

It is important to note that the purpose of the session is to raise children's self-esteem and provide an opportunity for children to acknowledge and celebrate their strengths and talents. This topic helps children to understand the importance of celebrating who they are rather than focusing on their appearance and their possessions. Teachers delivering this session must be aware that sensitivity should be shown when asking children to describe their strengths, as some who have low self-esteem for a variety of reasons are not used to describing themselves in this way, and may find it difficult, and in some cases painful, to identify their own strengths. Some children also may not have the vocabulary to describe their strengths. To address both of these areas of need, *My bounce back muscles* activity sheets have been devised to guide children through the session with additional word lists to encourage and support them.

Some children, particularly those with low self-esteem, may also need an adult to support them in the process of identifying their strengths and encouraging them to have a positive reflection of themselves. As noted throughout the programme, receiving positive recognition from an adult or from a peer can provide an important first step in enabling children to feel more positive about themselves.

It will be important for the teacher to emphasise to the class that each child should complete the *Bounce back muscles quiz* individually (unless of course additional adult support has been allocated to a child) and that the results of the quiz should be confidential and not shared with their peers.

Learning objectives

We are learning to:

- recognise our strengths

- understand what it means to be resilient.

Learning outcomes

I can:

- name my strengths

- tell you how my bounce back muscles can help me to be resilient.

Resources

Activity for class discussion:

- My bounce back muscles

Right Now activity:

- My bounce back muscles quiz

Extension activities:

- My bounce back shield

- My bounce back muscles record sheet

- Storyboarding – bounce back: bounce forward

Take Away activity:

- Look the part: the high-power pose

Key vocabulary

- bounce back muscles

- resilience
- qualities
- strengths

Pre-teaching session

Children with special educational needs and disabilities may benefit from a short pre-teaching session to introduce them to the key vocabulary that is used in this session. (For guidance on differentiation see page 62.)

INTRODUCTION (APPROX. 10 MINS)

- Open the session by reviewing the class rules that were agreed in the previous session. Is there anything that we might like to change, amend or add before we begin the session? Remind pupils of the reasons for having rules and how they can support their learning.

- Carry out random pairing so that each child has a Talk Partner for the session. (For guidance on how to make random pairings see page 59.)

- Review the Take Away activity from the previous session.

In this session we are going to be thinking about being resilient. Write the word *resilient* on the board.

Talk Partner discussion (approx. 5 mins)

- With their Talk Partner, ask the children to explore what they understand by the word *resilient* and if they know anyone who is *resilient*.

- Randomly choose a child to feed back to the class on this discussion.

Starter activity: Mind Map: resilience (approx. 5 mins)

Ask each child to create a Mind Map around the word *resilience*.

Class discussion: What is resilience? (approx. 15 mins)

Explain to the class that, every day, many different things happen to us all. Some of these things make us feel happy; some can make us feel sad or angry. Some things can challenge us. Resilience is about the way that we react when these things happen to us. Being resilient means 'bouncing back' from tricky situations.

Share and explain the learning objectives and outcomes with the class.

Talk Partner activity (approx. 10 mins)

With their Talk Partner, ask the children to take it in turns to make up a short story that describes a tricky situation that somebody, i.e. *not them*, found themselves in and how they reacted. Were they resilient? If yes, what helped that person to be resilient? (For guidance on using distancing techniques see page 51.)

Randomly choose a child to share their story. Check with the class whether they agree that the example accurately reflects what it means to be resilient.

Class discussion continued (approx. 10 mins)

Being resilient is a skill that we can learn. There are four special muscles that can help us to feel strong. We call these special muscles our bounce back muscles. Just like the muscles in our body, the more we use our bounce back muscles the stronger they will become. Being able to bounce back from tricky situations is called being resilient.

Introduce the bounce back muscles. (Teachers may wish to distribute copies of the *My bounce back muscles* activity sheets to the class and particularly to children who they consider may have difficulty suggesting examples of the vocabulary that is required for this activity.)

There are four bounce back muscles.

1. The first bounce back muscle is 'I can'. 'I can' is about remembering our strengths; the things that we are good at. Ask the children to think about their 'I can' strengths, i.e. their talents and skills. Thinking about the activities that we are good at can help us to feel strong. Take feedback and record responses.

2. The second bounce back muscle is 'I have'. Our 'I have' muscle is all about all the people that we have in our life: our friends and family and all the people who we can count on. Remembering these people can help us to feel strong. Take feedback and record responses.

3. The third bounce back muscle is 'I am'. 'I am' muscles are all about our special qualities. Our strengths are the good things about us. When things are tricky or we are faced with a challenge, remembering these things can make us feel strong. Ask the class for examples of their 'I am' strengths. Take feedback and record responses.

4. The fourth bounce back muscle is 'I like'. 'I like' is about remembering the things that we enjoy doing. We may enjoy swimming, drawing, dancing or taking photographs. Remembering these enjoyable activities can make us feel positive and proud of ourselves. Happy memories remind us of the good times and help us to feel strong when we have to deal with tricky situations. Ask the class for examples of their 'I like' strengths. Take feedback and record responses.

Right Now activity: My bounce back muscles quiz (approx. 10 mins)

Distribute copies of the quiz for all members of the class to complete. It is important to be aware that some children for a variety of reasons may have low self-esteem, and an additional adult may need to assist them in completing this activity.

Mid-session learning stop (approx. 5 mins)

With their Talk Partners, ask the class to:

- check with each other how they are getting on with completing the quiz

- share any new ideas about what they have learnt so far in the lesson about resilience.

Randomly choose a child to feed back on this discussion, and then ask the remainder of the class for any further comments on the same points. Allow the class time to complete the quiz.

Class discussion continued (approx. 5 mins)

Summarise the session by emphasising that our bounce back muscles make us strong and help us to be resilient. Being able to identify our strengths, remembering that we have family and friends who care for us, being able to recognise our skills and talents and have interests and hobbies can help us to feel good about ourselves and able to cope when things go wrong or when we get into tricky situations.

Extension activities

Distribute copies of the following activities to each child:

- *My bounce back shield:* Ask the class to decorate their protective shields with words or drawings from the Bounce back quiz. Explain that these shields are their internal 'armour' or protection that will help them to bounce back from tricky situations and bounce forward and take on new challenges.

- *My bounce back muscles record sheet:* Remind the class of the importance of continuing to build their bounce back muscles by noticing new strengths, finding new friends and discovering new hobbies and activities that they enjoy. Ask the class to use the My bounce back muscles record to add any new strengths that they learn about themselves as they progress through the programme.

- *Storyboarding – bounce back: bounce forward:* Ask the class to use the storyboarding framework to write and draw a story about a time when they remember their bounce back muscles helping them to bounce back from a tricky situation or to take on a new challenge and bounce forward.

Take Away activity: Look the part: the high-power pose (approx. 5 mins)

Explain that the high-power pose is a way of holding our bodies that helps us to show the world that we feel good about ourselves. The high-power pose increases our good feelings and our self-confidence. This is because it releases chemicals into our bodies that tell us that we are feeling good about ourselves. Low-power poses such as a hunched back and crossed arms have the opposite effect and make our brains release chemicals that can make us feel low.

Ask the class to stand and practise the high-power pose:

- Think about your strengths

- Stand tall

- Shoulders back and chest open

- Breathe slowly and deeply

- Keep your chin up and level

- Eyes straight ahead

- Slight smile

- Hands on hips

- Weight centred

- Feet slightly apart.

Remember your bounce back muscles and practise the high-power pose every day *and* whenever you need to feel strong, such as before a spelling or maths test or when you face a new challenge.

Final plenary: reflect and review (approx. 10 mins)

- Revisit the learning objectives and outcomes for the session with the class and discuss whether they have been met.

- With their Talk Partners, ask the class to talk through and then individually, with a different colour pen, add new learning and ideas to their *resilient* Mind Maps from the beginning of the session.

- Encourage the class to ask any questions that they have in relation to the session. Children who are able to communicate in writing can be encouraged to submit anonymous questions after the session by using the letter box.

- End the session with *Pass the smile* or another closure activity. (For guidance on closure activities see page 44.)

MY BOUNCE BACK MUSCLES

I am: My top five special qualities

Choose the top five words that describe you best.

Use the empty boxes if you want to add your own words.

Kind	Tidy	Loving	Proud
Cool	Thoughtful		Sensitive
Gentle	Quiet	Tough	Neat
Strong	Calm	Brave	
Healthy		Cheerful	Caring
Clever	Fun	Fair	
Friendly	Loyal	Generous	Fast
	Honest	Helpful	Responsible
Funny	Hard working	Musical	Likeable
Tidy		Artistic	

My top five:

1 _____

2 _____

3 _____

4 _____

5 _____

Copyright © Ruth MacConville 2017

✓

I can

Colour the boxes that name the things that you can do.

Use the empty boxes to add anything else that you can do.

Colouring	Reading
Write stories and/or poems	Tell funny jokes
Paint	Take care of pets
	Play football
Swim	Speak more than one language
Make friends	
	Keep friends
Draw	
Dance	
Help people	Ride a bike
Ice skate	
Sing	Cook

I like: My top five hobbies and interests

Make a list of the top five things that you enjoy doing.

1 _____

2 _____

3 _____

4 _____

5 _____

Copyright © Ruth MacConville 2017

I have

Draw a picture of yourself or write your name in the middle of the circle and then draw or write the names of the other people in your life in the other circles.

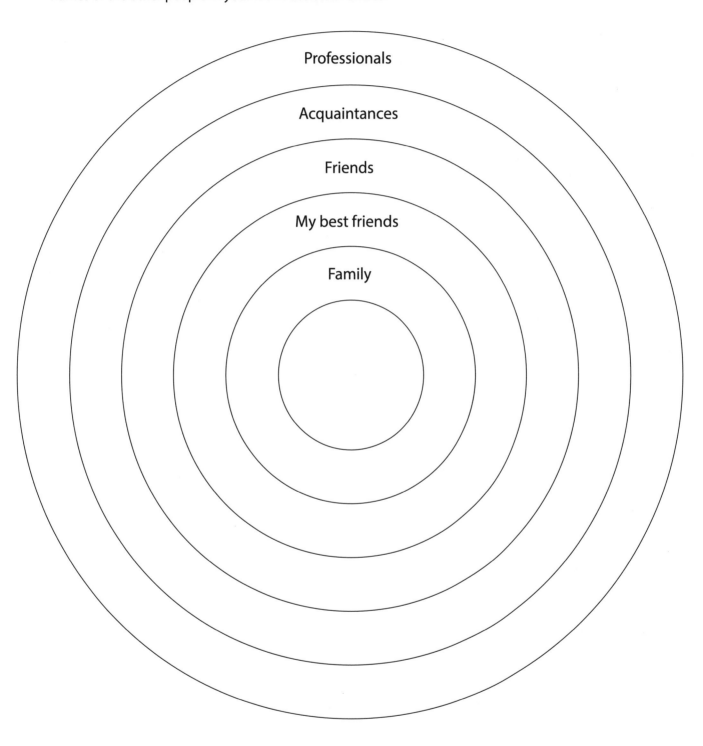

Professionals

Acquaintances

Friends

My best friends

Family

Copyright © Ruth MacConville 2017

Name: _____ Date: _____

MY BOUNCE BACK MUSCLES QUIZ

I have	Yes	No	I am	Yes	No
I have people around me whom I trust and who love me, no matter what			I am someone that people can like and love		
I have people who show me, by the way they do things, how to do things right			I am able to use my strengths every day		
I have people who want me to learn to do things on my own			I am willing to be responsible for what I do		
I have people who help me when I am upset, sick, in danger or need to learn something new			I am sure things will be all right		
I can	**Yes**	**No**	**I like**	**Yes**	**No**
I can talk to others about things that frighten or bother me			I like taking part in hobbies		
I can find ways to solve problems that I face			I like enjoying myself in fun situations		
I can control myself when I feel like doing something not right			I like doing nice things for others and showing my concern		
I can bounce back from difficult situations			I like having a laugh with my friends		

Add your 'yesses' for questions 1–4. This is your 'I have' muscle. My total is…

Add your 'yesses' for questions 5–8. This is your 'I am' muscle. My total is…

Add your 'yesses' for questions 9–12. This is your 'I can' muscle. My total is…

Add your 'yesses' for questions 13–16. This is your 'I like' muscle. My total is…

If you scored 3 or 4 on any muscle, well done.

If you scored below 3, it is time to build that muscle. Talk to your teacher about what you can do.

Copyright © Ruth MacConville 2017

Name: _____ Date: _____

MY BOUNCE BACK SHIELD

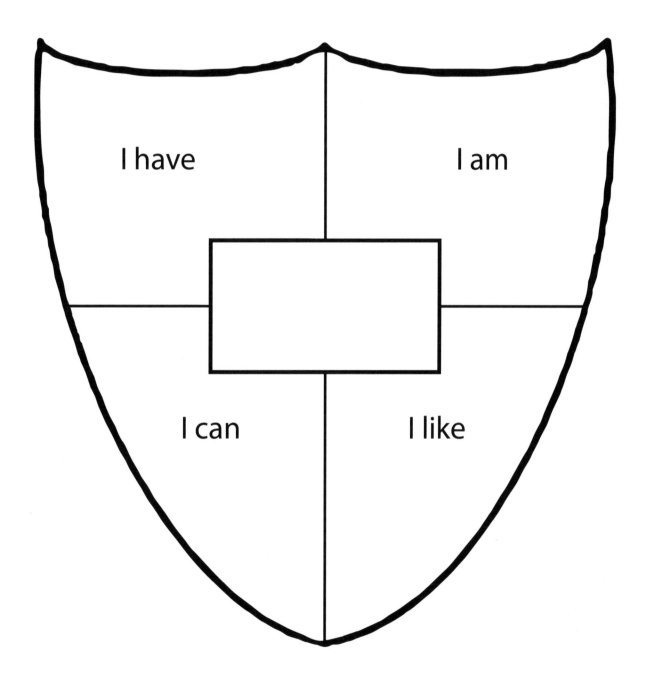

I have

I am

I can

I like

Copyright © Ruth MacConville 2017

✓

Name: _____ Date: _____

MY BOUNCE BACK MUSCLES RECORD SHEET

Use this record sheet to add any new strengths, skills, friends or hobbies that you discover during the programme.

Bounce back muscles	
I am (my positive personal qualities)	I have (my family and friends)
I can (my skills, abilities, talents)	I like (my hobbies and interests)

Copyright © Ruth MacConville 2017

Name: _____ Date: _____

STORYBOARDING – BOUNCE BACK: BOUNCE FORWARD

Write and draw a story about a time when you remember your bounce back muscles helping your character to bounce back from a tricky situation or helping you to take on a new challenge and bounce forward.

1. Where does your story take place?	2. What is the tricky situation your character faces?	3. Say some more.
4. What did your character decide to do?	5. Who will help?	6. How will they help?
7. How does your character solve the problem?	8. What has your character learnt?	9. How does your story end?

Copyright © Ruth MacConville 2017

LOOK THE PART: THE HIGH-POWER POSE

1. Draw a picture of yourself in the frame.

2. Use these phrases to label your picture:

Think about your strengths, Breathe deeply, Stand tall, Shoulders back, Chin up and level, Eyes straight ahead, Slight smile, Hands on hips, Feet slightly apart.

Remember:
Think about your strengths and practise the high-power pose every day, especially when you need to look the part and feel confident.

Copyright © Ruth MacConville 2017

SESSION 3: STRENGTHS SPOTTING
Background notes

'Strengths spotting' is a term coined by the positive psychologist Alex Linley (2008). Children who can identify their strengths and the things that they can do well rely less on their appearance and their possessions to determine their self-esteem. A study by the Search Institute in Minneapolis (Syvertsen, Roehlkepartain and Scales 2012), a non-profit organisation dedicated to discovering what children need to succeed, discovered that the great majority of children can, in fact, identify their 'sparks', i.e. the things in their lives that make them feel special, alive and real. It is extremely motivating for children to have their strengths acknowledged, and celebrating them has the potential to enable children to manage uncertain times and deal with the pressures that they are under from, for example, the social media with its promise of constant connectedness. In order to make the concept of strengths more accessible, this session is based on the concept of a 'strengths wardrobe' originally devised by Jenifer Fox (2009), an American educator and author. In this framework, learning strengths are represented by hats, relationship strengths by T-shirts, and activity strengths, i.e. practical skills and talents, by gloves and/or shoes.

Learning objectives

We are learning to:

- recognise our strengths
- understand the different types of strengths.

Learning outcomes

I can:

- name my strengths
- explain how my different strengths work together.

Resources

Circle Time activity:

- Strengths spotting

Right Now activity:

- My best time.

Take Away activity:

- At my very best

Key vocabulary

- strengths
- relationships
- learning
- activity
- heroine
- variety

Pre-teaching session

Children with special educational needs and disabilities may benefit from a short pre-teaching session to introduce them to the key vocabulary that is used in this session. (For guidance on differentiation see page 62.)

Introduction (approx. 10 mins)

- Open the session by reviewing the class rules that were agreed in the earlier session. Is there anything that we might like to change, amend or add before we begin the session? Remind pupils of the reasons for having rules and how they can support their learning.

- Carry out random pairing so that each child has a Talk Partner for the session. (For guidance on how to make random pairings see page 60.)

- Review the Take Away activity from the previous session.

Starter activity (approx. 5 mins)

Write the following sentence on the board:

Our appearance is only one part of who we are. True or False?

- With their Talk Partner, ask the children to think about the sentence and decide whether they think it is true or false.

- Ask Talk Partners to *snowball*, i.e. join up with two other Talk Partners to make a group of six, and find out how many think that the statement is true and how many think that it is false. Ask the group to discuss the reasons for their answers until they reach a consensus.

- Take feedback from each group and take a tally on how many children agree/disagree and how many are unsure.

Share the learning objectives and outcomes for the session with the class.

Circle Time activity: Strengths spotting (approx. 15 mins)

Although we all have strengths, sometimes it can be hard to spot them for ourselves. This is because we may not be used to thinking about ourselves in this way.

It is important to remember that sometimes it is difficult for children to identify their own strengths. Participating in a strengths spotting Circle Time activity provides an opportunity for the class to receive compliments from their peers. For many children, especially those with low self-esteem, receiving this recognition can provide an important step in the process of learning to feel good about themselves.

Remind the class that the class rules that operate during the sessions also apply to Circle Time.

The class sits in a circle and one child at a time takes a turn sitting in the middle. The child who is in the middle should not speak but should listen to the comments made by each member of the circle. Each child in the circle takes a turn sharing a positive comment or compliment about the person who is in the middle of the circle. Remind the class that the comments should not refer to a child's appearance or belongings; they should describe each individual's strengths and talents.

After each child in the circle shares a comment about the child in the middle, that child should say *thank you* and return to the circle. The next child can then take the seat in the centre. This process should be repeated until all members of the class have participated.

Whole-class discussion: A strengths wardrobe (approx. 10 mins)

We can think about our strengths in terms of a *strengths wardrobe*: a selection of hats, T-shirts and shoes/gloves. Just as everybody has their own wardrobe or collection of clothes, so everybody has their own wardrobe or collection of different sorts of strengths.

In our strengths wardrobe we have the following:

- Strengths hats: these are our learning strengths and they describe how we learn and how we think. We may have different hats or learning strengths for different occasions.

- Strengths T-shirts: these are our relationship strengths because we wear our T-shirts next to our heart. Just as we all have different T-shirts that we wear at different times, so we have to use different relationship strengths.

- Strengths shoes/gloves: these strengths are about our practical talents, about 'doing' and being active. Just as we all have different shoes/gloves that we wear at different times, we also have different activity strengths that we use at different times.

Revisit the list of strengths that were generated by the class during the introduction to the session and categorise them into learning, relationship and activity strengths.

The activity sheet *Strengths spotting* can be used as a prompt sheet for this discussion.

Right Now activity: My best time (approx. 10 mins)

With their Talk Partner, ask the children to take it in turns to describe 'my best time', a time when they felt at their very best. Each story should have:

- a beginning which sets the scene

- a middle which explains what happens in the story

- an end that brings the story to a close.

Ask children to listen carefully to their partner's story and spot their partner's learning, relationship and activity strengths. Use the activity sheet *My best time* to record these strengths.

Mid-session learning stop (approx. 5 mins)

Step 1

Randomly choose a child to feed back to the class on how they are getting on with this activity using the following questions:

- Were you able to follow your partner's story?

- Did the story have a clear structure: a beginning, middle and end?

- Could you identify your Talk Partner's learning, relationship and activity strengths?

- Is there anything else that you would like to add?

Step 2

Ask the remainder of the class to review how they are getting on with this activity in a similar way. Allow the class five minutes to complete the activity.

Extension activities

- Go on a strengths search: ask the class to talk to members of their family and their friends and discover new strengths. Make a list of these strengths.

- Think about your own strengths and how to use them in new ways.

- Find some books and poems that are about individuals who have special strengths, for example *The Hundred Dresses*, by Eleanor Estes (Houghton Mifflin Harcourt Publishing Company).

Take Away activity: At my very best (approx. 5 mins)

Introduce this activity that involves children thinking about themselves at their very best in three different situations and identifying the learning, relationship and activity strengths that they are using in each.

Final plenary: reflect and review (approx. 10 mins)

- Revisit the learning objectives and outcomes for the session with the class and discuss whether they have been met.

- With their Talk Partner, ask the class to talk through something new that they have learnt in the session.

- Review the learning of the class with a closing round asking each child to finish the sentence: *Something that I have learned that I did not know before...* The children's responses can be recorded by the teacher or a teaching assistant, written down by the children themselves.

- Encourage the class to ask any questions that they have in relation to the session. Children who are able to communicate in writing can be encouraged to submit anonymous questions after the session by using the question box.

- End the session with *Pass the smile* or a similar closure activity. (For guidance on closure activities see page 44.)

✓

Name: _____ Date: _____

STRENGTHS SPOTTING

Read the lists carefully and then add more strengths of your own in each of the sections.

Learning strengths

- Look
- Plan
- Listen
- Determined
- Concentrate
- Thinking
- Pay attention
-
-
-

- Curious
- Grit (Don't give up)
- Remember
- Have a go
- Keep improving
- Use your imagination: think up new ideas and ask new questions
- Enjoy your learning!
-
-
-

Relationship strengths

- Kind
- Thoughtful
- Loving
- Helpful
-
-
-

- Patient
- Loyal
- Hardworking
- Co-operative
-
-
-

Copyright © Ruth MacConville 2017

Activity strengths

- Drawing
- Painting
- Writing
- Cooking
- Counting
- Sewing
- Reading
- Talking
-
-
-

- Swimming
- Running
- Walking
- Helping
- Dancing
- Singing
- Diving
-
-
-
-

Copyright © Ruth MacConville 2017

✓

Name: _____ Date: _____

MY BEST TIME

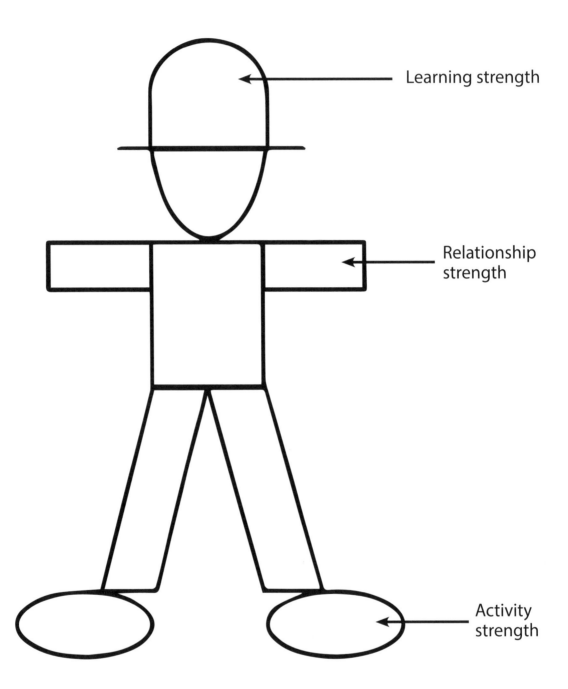

Learning strength

Relationship strength

Activity strength

Copyright © Ruth MacConville 2017

Name: _____ Date: _____

AT MY VERY BEST

Remember three times when you felt at your very best.

Write about or draw them in the three boxes below.

Then list the different strengths you were using on each occasion.

1.	Learning strength Relationship strength Activity strength
2.	Learning strength Relationship strength Activity strength
3.	Learning strength Relationship strength Activity strength

Copyright © Ruth MacConville 2017

SESSION 4: HERE AND NOW

Background notes

The purpose of this session is to introduce children to the practice of mindfulness.

> Mindfulness means maintaining a moment-by-moment awareness of our thoughts, feelings, bodily sensations and surrounding environment. Mindfulness also involves acceptance, meaning that we pay attention to our thoughts and feelings without judging them – without believing, for instance, that there's a 'right' or 'wrong' way to think or feel in a given moment. When we practice mindfulness, our thoughts tune in to what we're experiencing in the present moment rather than rehashing the past or imagining the future. (Greater Good Science Center, quoted in Brown 2015, p.71)

Mindfulness may have become one of the latest buzzwords, but it has a 2,600-year-old track record as a simple and practical set of skills that can transform our daily lives. In her article 'Mindfulness', Sally Turner (2014) writes that the practice is increasingly recognised in Western psychology as an effective way of reducing stress, and enhancing focus, self-awareness and emotional well-being. Mindfulness is not simply an abstract body of knowledge but a practical set of skills that can increase children's life skills by enabling them to become more fully aware of living right now, in the present moment.

According to the Mindfulness in Schools Project (undated), one of the easiest ways to get into a mindful state is to simply sit down on a chair, close your eyes and begin to focus on your breathing. As you sit still, relaxed but also alert, you can then direct your attention to the sensation of each inhalation and exhalation, and also become aware of the feeling of air as it enters and then leaves your mouth or nostrils. It is while you are doing this that other thoughts will enter into your mind. The idea is to become more aware of these intrusive thoughts, noting each of these in turn, without judgement, and then simply letting them pass. This is one of the key elements of mindfulness and the skill that is focused on throughout the session. Mindfulness can also be practised in everyday activities, from cleaning our teeth to walking, listening and eating. The key is to experience each moment fully by becoming aware of the sensations in our body, the sounds around us and the thoughts and feelings that are arising.

Engaging children with attention difficulties in mindfulness activities requires an approach that takes into account their shorter attention span. Sessions of just a few minutes, such as practising breathing exercises or listening mindfully to the sound of a bell, can be effective in enabling them to be present in the here and now.

To be effective, mindfulness needs to be practised daily both at home and integrated into children's daily lives as a habit of awareness. We can encourage children to practise carrying out everyday tasks – such as brushing their teeth, dressing and eating mindfully – with their full attention.

In this session, children are introduced to mindfulness and practise bringing their full attention to the here and now using everyday activities such as 'box breathing', looking around them and really seeing their surroundings, carefully listening to the sounds around them. The different ways to build mindfulness into their everyday lives are also explored.

Learning objectives

We are learning to:

- pay attention to our breathing
- practise being present in the here and now.

Learning outcomes

I can practise:

- paying attention to my breathing
- being present in the here and now.

Resources

A glass jar, a handful of sand or soil, water.

Mindfulness activity:

- Box breathing

Take Away activity:

- My mindfulness diary

KEY VOCABULARY

- present
- breathing
- calm
- practise
- mindfulness

Pre- teaching Session

- Children with special educational needs and disabilities may benefit from a short pre-teaching session to introduce them to the key vocabulary that is used in this session. (For guidance on differentiation see page 62.)

Introduction (approx. 10 mins)

- Open the session by reviewing the class rules that were agreed in the earlier session. Is there anything that we might like to change, amend or add before we begin this session? Remind pupils of the reasons for having rules and how they can support their learning.

- Carry out random pairing so that each child has a Talk Partner for the session (see page 59 for guidance on how to make these pairings).

- Review the Take Away activity from the previous session.

- Explain that this session is going to be about learning how to be calm by practising mindfulness. Mindfulness means having a regular, quiet time by calming our minds, relaxing our bodies and bringing all of our attention to what's happening in the here and now.

- Explain to the class that each morning in school when the register is called, children let the teacher know that they are present. However, although our bodies may be in the classroom, our thoughts might be somewhere else. We might be thinking about something else.

Talk Partner discussion (approx. 5 mins)

Ask the children to discuss with their Talk Partner whether this is true for them. Are there times when they should be paying attention but find themselves thinking about something else? Randomly choose a child to feed back on this discussion.

Share the learning objectives and learning outcomes for the session with the class.

Mindful Monkey, Happy Panda

A short story adapted from *Mindful Monkey, Happy Panda* by Lauren Alderfer and Kerry Lee MacLean (2011) can help to explain the importance of paying attention to the present moment and not letting our thoughts wander away from what we are doing.

One day Monkey met Panda and asked him an important question: 'You always seem so happy and peaceful, what do you do to be like that?'

Panda said, 'I walk, I work, I read, I eat, I play and I rest.'

Monkey said, 'I walk, I work, I read, I eat, I play and I rest too, but I am not happy and peaceful like you.'

Panda asked Monkey, 'What do you think about when you do those things?'

Monkey replied, 'When I read I think about eating, when I'm eating I think about playing, when I play I think about resting, and when I'm resting I think about walking.'

'Ah,' said Happy Panda, 'your monkey mind jumps from one thing to another and it's always somewhere other than here, to something other than what you're doing right now.'

'Well, of course it does,' said Monkey. 'Isn't that what everyone's mind does?'

'Well,' said Happy Panda, 'when I walk I'm just walking, when I work I'm just working, when I read I'm just reading, when I eat I'm just eating and when I play I'm just playing.' Happiness, says Happy Panda, comes from bringing all your attention to whatever you are doing right now. It is about being mind-full, like your mind is full of the present, full of right now.

From that moment Monkey started to practise mindfulness.

Mid-session learning stop (approx. 5 mins)

With their Talk Partners, ask the class to talk together about the story and what they have learnt from it. Randomly choose a child to share what they have learnt and their comments on the story.

Practising mindfulness (approx. 10 mins)

Explain to the class that we are now going to practise being mindful just like the Happy Panda. This means that we are going to practise making sure that our mind is full of the present – the here and now.

Note: Breathing is central to practising mindfulness. The breathing activity many mindfulness practitioners teach is 'square' or 'box' breathing. They use it for increasing mindfulness and decreasing anxiety and stress. Square or box breathing provides a useful introduction to the practice of mindfulness.

Square or box breathing

Explain to the class that, when we are nervous or stressed, our breathing becomes shallow and fast. Certain ways of breathing can help us to become calm and to focus. Try this:

- Breathe in to a count of four seconds.
- Hold for a count of four seconds.
- Breathe out to a count of four seconds.
- Hold to a count of four seconds.
- Do this three more times.

Keep calm

This four-step breathing activity is a useful introduction to the practice of mindfulness.

1. Tell yourself, 'Stop and take a look around.'
2. Tell yourself, 'Keep calm.'

3. Take a deep breath through your nose while you count to five, hold it while you count to two, and then breathe out through your mouth while you count to five.

4. Repeat these steps until you feel calm.

(Adapted from Elias, Tobias and Friedlander 1999)

At this point in the session, teachers should select the most appropriate mindfulness activities for their class to practise from those listed below.

Three senses activity

This activity helps children to notice what they are experiencing right now through three senses: sound, sight and touch.

First ask the children to take a few slow breaths and ask themselves:

- What are the three things that I can hear?

- What are the three things I can see?

- What are the three things I can feel?

Now ask the children to slowly repeat this activity choosing different items to focus on.

Note: It's impossible to do this exercise and not be present and mindful.

Mind in a jar

This activity is useful for children who are new to mindfulness, as the process involves movement that has the capacity to hold the children's attention.

- Fill a glass jar with water and notice how it's like one's mind during a quiet moment – clean and clear, like the sky.

- The next step is to take a small handful of sand or soil and place it in the jar. Ask the children to imagine that each one of the tiny grains represents one of their thoughts. Some are sad, some are exciting, some are angry.

- Put the lid on the jar and shake it up, so that everything swirls around faster and faster.

- Ask the children to imagine that this is like your mind in a hurry, with lots of thoughts swirling around.

- Now let the jar calm down by placing it on a table. Explain to the class that this is how our mind calms down during mindfulness. Watch the thoughts settle down to the bottom of the jar, leaving the water – your mind – light and clear, instead of dark and cloudy. Explain to the class that now they can act peacefully because they can think clearly.

(Adapted from MacLean, 2004)

A game of I-Spy

Remind the class that I-Spy is a guessing game where one person describes something that they *spy* in the classroom and the rest of the class guess what that something is that the person is looking at.

- Explain that the importance of this game is not to win or lose, but to look really carefully and notice what's in the room.

- Choose an object in the room such as a clock which is easily visible to the whole class and describe it:

  ◦ I spy with my little eye…something round and white.

- Add more details if the class need it, for example it's about as big as a dinner plate, until the children guess what you are looking at.

- Play a few rounds of I-Spy with the teacher describing the object and the class guessing what it is.

- Then choose a child to 'spy' an object and the rest of the class guess what it is.

- Ask the class to reflect on the activity:

  ◦ Did you notice anything in the room that you hadn't noticed before?

  ◦ What did you notice?

- Explain that what the class was doing in this I-Spy game was *seeing* mindfully.

Talk Partner discussion (approx. 5 mins)

With their Talk Partners, ask the class to think about how they felt during these activities. Randomly choose a child to feed back on the discussion.

Class discussion (approx. 10 mins)

Explain that we can do lots of things mindfully, or with our minds full of the present. Being mindful means that we are paying full attention with all our senses to what we are doing in the moment. We can brush our hair, clean our teeth, wash our hands, eat our food, read a book, take a drink or go for a walk mindfully.

Take Away activities

Explain the following activities to the class:

- Ask the children to practise mindfulness during the coming week and record their experience on their mindfulness diaries.

- Practise taking mindfulness breaks, using the square or box breathing activity.

- Practise the Mind in a jar activity at home or use a snow globe. Suggest that children shake the globe and imagine that those little snow particles are all the thoughts in their minds. Watch the globe carefully until all the snow settles to the bottom, leaving their minds as clear as the water.

Final plenary: reflect and review (approx. 10 mins)

- Revisit the learning objectives and outcomes for the session and discuss with the class whether they have been met.

- Encourage the class to ask any questions that they have in relation to the session. Children who are able to communicate in writing can be encouraged to submit anonymous questions after the session by using the letter box.

- With their Talk Partners, ask the class to talk through something new that they have learnt in the session.

- Review the learning of the class with a closing round asking each child to finish the sentence: *Something that I have learned that I did not know before...* The children's responses can be recorded by the teacher or a teaching assistant, or written down by the children themselves.

- End the session with *Pass the smile* or a similar closure activity. (For guidance on closure activities see page 44.)

BOX BREATHING

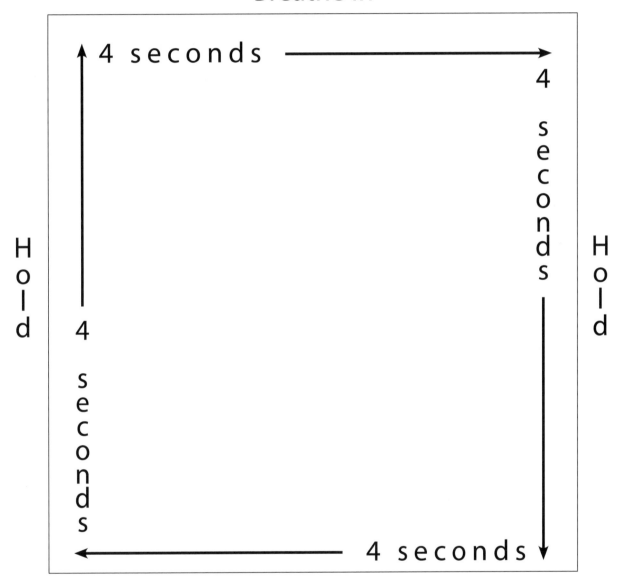

Copyright © Ruth MacConville 2017

✓

Name: _____ Date: _____

MY MINDFULNESS DIARY

Remember to practise mindfulness activities as often as you can. Spending a few minutes each day practising breathing exercises can help to make them part of your daily routine. Note down on the diary what activities you tried, when you tried them and how they felt. Give each activity a score out of five. Use the boxes below to record the times that you practised being mindful.

When/Date	Where?	What did I do?	How did I feel?	Score

Copyright © Ruth MacConville 2017

SESSION 5: THE REAL YOU

It is important for teachers to be aware that this session may raise sensitive issues if there are children in the class who for a variety of reasons are particularly vulnerable because of their family background. These may include children who have been adopted or who are in the local authority care system and also those children who for a variety of reasons do not know their biological parents. These children may not wish to take part in the session, and their decision should be respected. It is crucial that all staff are sensitive to the needs and experiences of individual children and make them aware of the sources of support both inside and outside school. (For guidance on dealing with sensitive issues see page 53.)

Background notes

This session explores the fact that we are all genetically predisposed to inherit many of our body features from our parents and grandparents and that our genes are the biggest influence on our body shape and size. Activities and discussion on this theme will lead on to an exploration of body shape diversity, the importance of celebrating the fact that we are all different, and what we can do to look after ourselves and keep healthy.

During this discussion children may express a preference for certain body sizes and shapes. It will be important to convey that although the choices of what we eat and how much we exercise can influence our weight and shape, in fact our genes limit the extent that we can do this. It is important to accept how we look and to put energy into looking after ourselves.

Learning objectives

We are learning to:

- understand how our genes programme how we look

- appreciate the importance of respecting and looking after our bodies because of all the things that the body can do.

Learning outcomes

I can:

- recognise that there is a limit to how much we can control our appearance

- explain why it is important to look after my body because of all the things that it can do.

Resources

Right Now activity:

- All about me

Class activity:

- True/False cards: a sheet of A4 paper divided into 2 halves with 'true' written in one half and 'false' in the other. Children can make these for themselves.

Extension activities:

- My family tree

- Healthy habits: looking after ourselves

Take Away activity:

- Celebrate all the things your body can do

Key vocabulary

- replacement

- genes

- influence

- appreciate

- programme

- celebrate

Pre-teaching session

Children with special educational needs and disabilities may benefit from a short pre-teaching session to introduce them to the key vocabulary that is used in this session. (For guidance on differentiation see page 62.)

Introduction (approx. 10 mins)

- Open the session by reviewing the class rules that were agreed earlier. Is there anything that we might like to change, amend or add before we begin the session? Reiterate the reasons for having rules and how they can support their learning.

- Carry out random pairing so that each child has a Talk Partner for the session. (For guidance on random pairings see page 60.)

- Review the Take Away activities from the previous session. Write the following key messages on the board:
  - Your body is yours.
  - There are no replacement parts.
  - Take care of your body because you will have it for a long time.

With their Talk Partners, ask the class to discuss what these key messages mean to them.

Starter activity: Draw and Write activity: Your body is yours (approx. 5 mins)

Ask each child to describe what this statement means by drawing a picture and using words and/or writing notes to explain it. (For guidance on Draw and Write activities see page 41.)

Class discussion (approx. 10 mins)

Discuss with the class that the shape of our body – our basic frame – is something that we're born with, just like the shape of our nose and the colour of our eyes. Some people are tall and thin, while others are short and sturdy. Usually our body shape is like the shape of other members of our family. No one body type is better or worse than another. Everyone, whatever their body shape, can be fit, healthy and beautiful.

Talk Partner activity (approx. 10 mins)

- With their Talk Partners, ask the children to work in pairs and discuss the aspects of their appearance that:
  - can be changed, for example our hairstyle, our way of dressing
  - can't be changed, for example height, skin colour, bone structure, colour of eyes.

Ask the Talk Partners to snowball or join up with two other Talk Partners to make a group of six children and together compare their answers and create a two-part group list.

Class discussion (approx. 15 mins)

- Take feedback on this activity and scribe the group's responses in two lists:
  - things that we can change about our appearance
  - things that we can't change.

Note: During this discussion children may suggest that they can change their body shape by dieting, exercise or even cosmetic surgery. It will be important to emphasise that there is a limit to how much we can permanently change our body shape in these ways. It may also be necessary to talk to the class about the risks and disadvantages of cosmetic surgery.

Class discussion (approx. 15 mins)

Explain to the class that there is a limit to how much we can change our bodies. This is because of our genes. Our genes are inherited from our parents and grandparents and they programme our bodies, i.e. tell our bodies how to grow.

The colour of our skin, the shape of our nose and the curliness of our hair are all programmed by a set of instructions, which are called our genes. The information in our genes comes from our mother, our father and our grandparents, which is probably why we all tend to look a little bit like both our parents.

There are three important facts about our genes to explain to the class. Our genes are:

- like computers that programme our bodies how to grow

- inherited from our biological parents and grandparents

- responsible for at least 50 per cent of our body size and shape.

Many people think that the main thing that influences a person's size is how much we eat and how much we exercise, but our genes also influence us. Our genes are in place before we are born. Whether we are taller, shorter, fatter or thinner is built into our bodies before we are born and influences how we look.

Our genes are responsible for:

- our bone structure: the length, width and thickness of our bones. This means how long, short, thin and thick our bones are. This will affect our height, the length of our arms, our backbone, how wide our shoulders and hips are, how big our feet will grow, the shape of our nose, and lots more

- how much fat is stored in our body

- where fat is stored in our body

- how quickly or slowly we burn up our food.

Talk Partner discussion (approx. 5 mins)

With their Talk Partners, ask the class to explore who they look like in their own families. Emphasise the fact that many of us take after a number of our relatives; we may even take after our grandparents or our great grandparents. Suggest children explore how the various aspects of their appearance – height, hair texture and colour, eye shape and colour, skin colouring, size of hands and feet – are like other members of their family.

Also ask the class to explore how their strengths, interests, talents and hobbies can also be 'inherited' from members of their family.

Right Now activity: All about me (approx. 10 mins)

Introduce and talk through this activity with the class.

Mid-session learning stop (approx. 5 mins)

Step 1

Randomly choose a child to feed back to the class on how they are getting on with this activity.

Step 2

Ask the remainder of the class to also review how they are getting on with this activity. Allow the class five minutes to complete the activity.

Class activity

- Distribute a True/False card to the class. Read out the following statements and ask each child to respond by choosing a True or False card:
  ○ A lot of the way I look was determined (in place) before I was born.
  ○ While we may prefer to be a different body shape, it is important to celebrate who we are born to be.
  ○ Healthy eating and fitness habits can influence our weight and body shape, but our appearance is also influenced by our genes.

- Take a tally after each of the three sentences are read to ensure that the class have understood the importance of the effect of genes on their appearance.

Extension activities

- My family tree

- Healthy habits: looking after ourselves

- Read more about how your body works: *Your Body is Brilliant: Body Respect for Children* by Sigrun Danielsdottir, published by Singing Dragon

  ○ Design a poster illustrating the wide variety of how human beings look.

Take Away activity: Celebrate all the things your body can do

Introduce and talk through this activity with the class.

Final plenary: reflect and review (approx. 10 mins)

- Revisit the learning objectives and outcomes for the session with the class and discuss whether they have been met.

- Encourage the class to ask any questions that they have in relation to the session. Children who are able to communicate in writing can be encouraged to submit anonymous questions after the session by using the letter box.

- With their Talk Partners, ask the class to talk through what they have learnt in the session and then individually, with a different colour pen, add any new learning and ideas to the Draw and Write starter activity from the beginning of the session.

End the session with *Pass the smile* or a similar closure activity. (For guidance on closure activities see page 44.)

✓

Name: _____ Date: _____

ALL ABOUT ME

All about me	Who in your family has this too?
My hair colour is	
My hair is (curly or straight)	
My eyes are	
Draw your nose	
My skin colour is	
My strengths are	
My talents are	
My interests are	
Anything else	

Copyright © Ruth MacConville 2017

Name: _____ Date: _____

MY FAMILY TREE

Start at the bottom and put your name in the first box.

Write the names of your parents, then your grandparents and then your great grandparents in the boxes above. Add a few words about each person that describes something about how they look and what they are like. If you have never met some of them, ask another family member to help you.

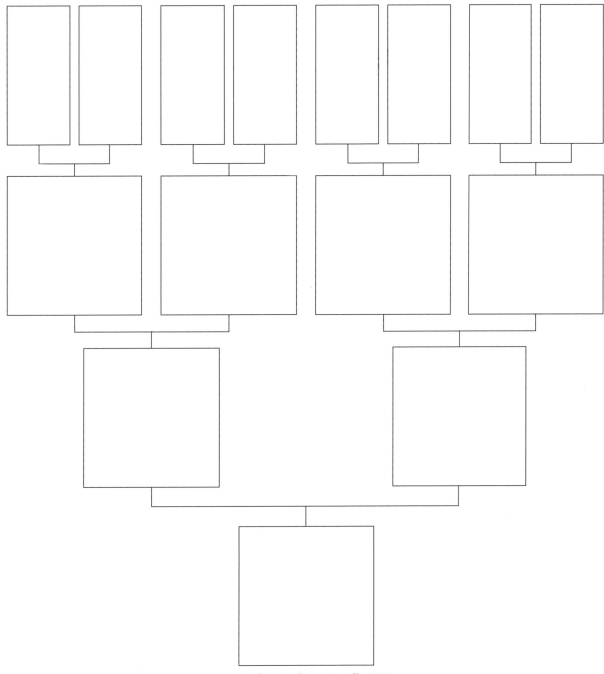

Copyright © Ruth MacConville 2017

✓

Name: _____ Date: _____

HEALTHY HABITS: LOOKING AFTER OURSELVES

Healthy habits are the things we do regularly to look after ourselves.

Think about how often you do these habits and colour one box in each line.

Habits	More than daily	Daily	Weekly	Monthly
Cleaning my teeth				
Brushing my hair				
Washing my hands				
Washing my face				
Having a shower/bath				
Having a haircut				
Having my finger nails cut				
Having my toe nails cut				
Choosing the right clothes to wear				

Copyright © Ruth MacConville 2017

Name: _____ Date:_____

CELEBRATE ALL THE THINGS YOUR BODY CAN DO

Your body is a work in progress. Think about all the things that it can do.

Draw a picture of yourself in the middle of the page.

In the boxes write the names of all your body parts that are useful to you.

Copyright © Ruth MacConville 2017

SESSION 6: HEALTHY EATING HABITS: THREE TO REMEMBER
Background notes

Good health is central to having a positive body image and feeling good about ourselves. It fosters positive moods and provides energy for our daily lives. This session introduces the concept of 'intuitive' or mindful eating, an approach that encourages the practice of enjoying or 'savouring' our food, i.e. paying attention to what we are eating and also listening to our body signals that tell us when we are hungry and also when we have had enough to eat. The work of paediatrician Susan L. Johnson (2000) has shown that it is possible to teach children how to become better at responding to their own internal fullness and suggests that the ability to stop eating when you are full is not genetic but is fundamentally a response to the environment and can therefore be learned. Johnson demonstrated that over six weeks of intervention it was possible to train children to improve their ability to self-regulate the amount of food they ate.

Learning objectives

We are learning to:

- understand healthy eating habits
- practise 'mindful' eating.

Learning outcomes

I can:

- tell you about healthy eating habits
- practise 'savouring' food or 'mindful' eating
- recognise my body signals that tell me when I am hungry and when I have had enough to eat.

Resources

Two raisins or pieces of other small fruit for each child.

Right Now activities:

- Eat a mix of foods every day
- Healthy eating habits

Extension activities:

- Is eating a pastime or a pleasure for you?
- I am hungry
- I am full up

Take Away activity:

- My food diary

Key vocabulary

- mindful
- intuitive
- variety
- savouring
- signals

Pre-teaching session

Children with special educational needs and disabilities may benefit from a short pre-teaching session to introduce them to the key vocabulary that is used in this session. (For guidance on differentiation see page 62.)

Introduction (approx. 10 mins)

- Open the session by reviewing the class rules that were agreed in the earlier session. Is there anything that we might like to change, amend or add before we begin the session? Remind pupils of the reasons for having rules and how they can support their learning.

- Carry out random pairing so that each child has a Talk Partner for the session. (For guidance on making random pairings see page 60.)

- Review the Take Away activity from the previous session.

- Write the words *healthy eating habits* on the board and ask the children to suggest what this means. Record their responses.

Starter activity: Draw and Write: Healthy eating habits

Ask each child to 'Draw and Write' their thoughts and ideas on healthy eating habits. (For guidance on Draw and Write activities see page 41.)

Class discussion (approx. 10 mins)

Introduce the idea that there are three main healthy eating habits to remember.
Healthy eating means:

- enjoying a mix of foods

- enjoying or 'savouring' our food

- listening to our body when it tells us when we are hungry and when we have had enough to eat.

1 Enjoying a mix of foods

Introduce the five main food groups:

- Vegetables

- Fruit

- Bread and cereals

- Milk and dairy foods

- Meat, fish, eggs, nuts, seeds, tofu.

Right Now activity: Eat a mix of foods every day (approx. 10 mins)

- Distribute a copy of the *Eat a mix of foods every day* activity sheet to each child.

- Ask Talk Partners to *snowball*, i.e. join up with two other Talk Partners. There should be at least five groups altogether.

- Allocate a food category to each group. Ask each group to brainstorm and list as many types of food that they can for their category.

- Take feedback from each group and ask for any further suggestions for each category from the class. Compile a list for each food category.

Class discussion (approx. 10 mins)

Explain that enjoying (or savouring) our food also means paying attention to what we are eating with each of our senses: how our food looks, feels, smells and tastes, as well as how we feel during and after eating.

2 Savouring food: The raisin exercise (approx. 10 mins)

This introduces the class to *savouring* or enjoying their food by paying attention to what they are eating.

Start by distributing two raisins to each child. Set a timer for three minutes and explain that, at first, this is going to seem like a very long time. Remind the class of the importance of doing this activity in slow motion and making it last for three minutes without speaking. Give the following instructions to the class:

- Take one of the raisins and hold it in your hand.

- Look carefully at the fruit and take your time to very carefully appreciate its shape, colour and aroma. It may help to pretend that you are going to describe the raisin to some being from another planet who has never seen a raisin before.

- Be aware of any thoughts that may come into your head as you look at the raisin. Note that they are just thoughts and continue looking carefully at the raisin.

- Explore the raisin carefully with your eyes, your fingers and your nose.

- Notice the colour of the raisin and what it looks like – is it bumpy or smooth, or dry or moist?

- Bring the raisin to your nose. Does it have any smells?

- Ask yourself, is your full attention on this raisin in your hand?

- Then, when you are ready, place the raisin in your mouth. Do you notice your mouth watering? Continue to keep your attention on the raisin and also watch your thoughts.

- Are the thoughts looking forward to swallowing the raisin and eating another one, or are your thoughts still on the raisin in your mouth?

- Gently bite the raisin. Taste the flavour.

- Slowly chew the raisin while noting every sensation.

- As you swallow the raisin, first note the decision to swallow it. Then feel it slide down your throat into your tummy.

- Can you feel that your body is now exactly one raisin heavier than it was a few minutes ago?

(Adapted from Semple and Lee 2011)

Class discussion (approx. 10 mins)

Lead a guided discussion with the following questions:

- What did you notice during that activity?

- Any surprises?

- Was that hard or easy to do? Why?

- What did you learn during the activity that you had not noticed before?

- What did you notice about the colour, smell or taste of the fruit that you hadn't noticed before?

- Did you enjoy savouring your food?

3 Listening to our body's alarm clock

Explain that healthy eating also means paying attention to our body's alarm clock. This means knowing when our body:

- sends us hunger signals that tell us when it is time to eat

- sends us full-up signals that we have had enough to eat.

Explain that as babies we knew exactly when we had enough to eat. It is very difficult to make babies eat more food when they are full up. As we get older we may lose touch with our body's signals that tell us when we have had enough to eat. Our hunger is our body's alarm clock. It lets us know when it is time to eat; however, because we also get lots of other messages from all around us encouraging us to eat even when we're not hungry, we can easily forget to listen to our body's alarm clock.

Talk Partner discussion (approx. 5 mins)

With their Talk Partners, ask the class to list the things that tempt us to eat even when we may not be hungry. Randomly choose a child to feed back on their discussion.

Class discussion (approx. 10 mins)

Explain that although many things may be tempting to eat, feeling hungry is different. It is important to listen to your body and eat when you're hungry and stop when you are full. Our hunger is a message that tells us that we need to eat.

Listening to our hunger can help us look after ourselves. It is good to eat mindfully and savour our food so we can recognise more easily when we are starting to feel we have eaten enough. If you want to look after your body, use your hunger as a guide to enjoy a mix of foods from the five food groups every day.

Right Now activity: Healthy eating habits (approx. 15 mins)

Distribute a copy of *Healthy eating habits* to each child. Ask the children to sit with their Talk Partners and read out each rule in turn and together agree on the following:

- a helpful rule for classroom talk (colour the box green)

- not a helpful rule (colour the box red)

- not sure if it is a helpful rule or not (colour the box orange)

- add two further rules that they think would be helpful.

Mid-session learning stop (approx. 5 mins)

Step 1

Randomly choose a child so that the whole class is focused as they do not know who will be selected.

Ask the child to explain:

- where they are up to with completing the task

- the rules that they have agreed that are helpful, the rules that are not helpful, the rules that they are unsure about and any new rules they have added

- how they went about making these decisions.

Step 2

Ask the rest of the class to reflect on their work in a similar way. Allow time for the class to complete the activity and then *snowball*, i.e. join up with two other Talk Partners to make a group of six children. Each group should then complete a joint *Healthy eating habits* sheet by sharing and building on the original choices that the class made with their Talk Partners. Ask the groups to decide who will report back to the class.

Allow time for the groups to complete the task (approx. 5 mins).

Class discussion (approx. 10 mins)

Ask each group to report back on the healthy eating habits that they agreed on. Complete a tally chart so that the children can see which habits everyone agrees on. Decide on a set of approximately six healthy eating habits.

Extension activities

Continue to take a few moments every day to practise savouring food and mindful eating. Take your time to explore:

- the smell of your food

- how your food looks on the plate – its colours and shapes

- the texture of different foods

- the flavour of your favourite food in your mouth

- swallowing just a little bite of your favourite food

- enjoying your food by eating it very, very slowly, one small bite at a time.

Complete the *Is eating a pleasure or a pastime for you?* activity sheet. Also, practise listening to your body's alarm clock every day and use the activity sheets *I am hungry* and *I am full up* to record the times when you hungry and the times when you feel full up.

Take Away activity: My food diary

Introduce and explain the worksheet *My food diary*.

Final plenary: reflect and review (approx. 10 mins)

- Revisit the learning objectives for the session with the class and discuss whether the learning outcomes have been met.

- Encourage the class to ask any questions that they have in relation to the session. Children who are able to communicate in writing can be encouraged to submit anonymous questions after the session by using the question box.

- With their Talk Partners, ask the class to talk through what they have learnt in the session and then individually, using a different colour pen, add any new learning or ideas on healthy eating to the Draw and Write activity from the beginning of the session.

- Finish the session with *Pass the smile* or a similar closure activity. (For guidance on closure activities see page 44.)

Copyright © Ruth MacConville 2017

Name: _____ Date: _____

EAT A MIX OF FOODS EVERY DAY

Every day, eat a mix of foods from the five main food groups. Write the names of the food from each of the five groups in the boxes below.

Vegetables	Fruit	Bread and cereals

Milk and dairy	Meat, fish, eggs, nuts, tofu

Copyright © Ruth MacConville 2017

HEALTHY EATING HABITS WORKSHEET

Name:

Read the ideas in the shapes carefully and COLOUR:

GREEN – good ideas

RED – not good ideas

ORANGE – not sure

- Make up two good ideas of your own. Write them in the circles.

1. Enjoy your food

2. Drink water

4. Listen to your body clock

3. Eat a mix of food every day

5. Eat while you are watching TV

6. Only eat your favourite foods

7. Eat when you are bored

8. Eat the same food every day

9. Forget to eat breakfast

Copyright © Ruth MacConville 2017

Name: _____ Date: _____

IS EATING A PLEASURE OR A PASTIME FOR YOU?

Read the sentences below and circle True or False for each one.

1. I eat when I am bored.   True   False

2. Snacks and TV always go together for me.   True   False

3. I reach into the biscuit tin, out of habit, whether I am hungry or not.   True   False

4. I reach into the fridge to find something to eat whether I am hungry or not.   True   False

5. I only eat when I am hungry.   True   False

6. I stop eating when I feel full up.   True   False

7. I eat when I am nervous.   True   False

8. I eat when I see my favourite food whether I am hungry or not.   True   False

Give yourself one mark for each time you said False to questions 1, 2, 3, 4, 7, 8. _____

Give yourself one mark for each time you said True to questions 5, 6.   _____

If you scored a total of four or more marks – well done! Eating is a pleasure for you, not a pastime.

If you scored less than four marks – practise listening to your body clock so that eating is a pleasure for you.

Copyright © Ruth MacConville 2017

✓

Name: _____ Date: _____

I AM HUNGRY

Listen to your body signals that tell you that you are hungry and need to eat.

Day	Time	How hungry am I?										
		0	1	2	3	4	5	6	7	8	9	10
		Starving					OK					Full

←——————————————————————————————→

Copyright © Ruth MacConville 2017

Name: _____ Date: _____

I AM FULL UP

Listen to your body signals that tell you when you have had enough to eat.

What time did I eat?	What did I eat?	How full am I?										
		0	1	2	3	4	5	6	7	8	9	10
		Starving				OK				Full		

←——————————————————→

Copyright © Ruth MacConville 2017

Name: _____ Date: _____

MY FOOD DIARY

Eat a variety of foods – mostly fruits and vegetables.

Colour the boxes each day when you eat food from the different groups – if on Monday you eat an apple, then colour the fruit box.

Eat a variety of foods so that you can colour five boxes every day.

My week	Vegetables	Fruit	Bread and cereals	Milk and dairy	Meat, fish, eggs, nuts, tofu
Monday					
Tuesday					
Wednesday					
Thursday					
Friday					
Saturday					
Sunday					

Copyright © Ruth MacConville 2017

SESSION 7: GET MOVING

Background notes

Note: During this lesson, it will be important to be sensitive to children who may have physical impairments that might limit some of the activities that they can do. Be ready to suggest that these children join in with the groups who are exploring activities that they can do and are comfortable with.

A report from the Chief Medical Officer, *At Least Five a Week: Evidence of the Impact of Physical Activity and its Relationship to Health* (Department of Health 2004), emphasises that exercise is vital for a child's healthy development. Children and young people should do a minimum of 60 minutes of physical activity each day. At least twice a week this should include more vigorous, aerobic exercise such as running, skipping, cycling or dancing. As children are up to their eyes in electronic media and with reduced opportunities for playing outdoors, Brooks (2006) writes that many children now lead sedentary lives.

Throughout childhood, children should continue to develop their physical strength and skills, but if, for example, their weight or lack of opportunity prevents them from keeping up with the sporting prowess of their peers, they are likely to become frustrated. Childhood is an important time for establishing healthy habits and celebrating a positive body image. This session encourages children to get moving in order to discover the activities and sports that they enjoy.

Learning objectives

We are learning to:

- identify different categories of movement
- understand why being active is important.

Learning outcomes

I can:

- explain why moving is important for my health
- tell you about the different types of movement
- practise making activity a daily habit.

Resources

Right Now activity:

- the five categories of movement

Extension activity:

- Visualise success

Take Away activity:

- My activity diary

Key vocabulary

- physical
- health
- types
- aerobic
- vigorous
- sedentary

Pre-teaching session

Children with special educational needs and disabilities may benefit from a short pre-teaching session to introduce them to the key vocabulary that is used in this session. (For guidance on differentiation see page 62.)

Introduction (approx. 10 mins)

- Open the session by reviewing the class rules that were agreed in the earlier session. Is there anything that we might like to change, amend or add before we begin the session? Remind pupils of the reasons for having rules and how they can support their learning.

- Carry out random pairing so that each child has a Talk Partner for the session. (For guidance on making these pairings see page 59.)

- Review the Take Away activity from the previous session.

- Write the following statement on the board:

  ◦ Children in this school should do more exercise.

- With their Talk Partners, ask the class whether they agree or disagree with this statement.

- Take a count on how many children agree/disagree and discuss their reasons as a class.

- Record their responses.

Starter activity

Distribute a piece of A4 plain paper to each child and ask them to mind-map everything they know about being active.

Class activity: Get moving (approx. 10 mins)

Place an *Agree* and a *Disagree* sign at opposite ends of the classroom and explain to the class that they need to listen carefully, and when they hear a statement they will need to choose which of the classroom to go to, depending on whether they agree with the statement or not.

Choose two children, one for each end of the room, to keep a tally on how many children agree or disagree with each of the following statements:

- Moving your body every day is your choice.

- Nobody can make you do it but you.

- Moving is a win-win situation.

- You'll feel better.

- Our body shapes our mind.

- Your brain will grow.

- You'll stay fit and healthy.

Talk Partner discussion (approx. 5 mins)

- With their Talk Partners, ask the class to discuss what they have learnt about the importance of *getting moving* from this activity.

- Randomly choose a child to feed back any new learning or questions from this activity.

Class discussion (approx. 10 mins)

Review the outcome of the tally for each of the seven statements with the class. Emphasise the following points to clarify the learning:

- It's up to each of us to be active every day in as many different ways that we can. Being active is our own choice.

- Being active makes us feel better, healthier and stronger, and it is also good for our brains.

- Being active helps us to learn because neuroscientists have discovered just how closely our body and our brain work together.

Now introduce the five categories of movement:

- Passive sitting

- Active sitting

- Everyday movement

- Vigorous movement

- Aerobic movement.

Right Now activity: The five categories of movement (approx 15 minutes)

Ask the Talk Partners to join up with two other Talk Partners. There should be five groups altogether. Allocate a category of movement to each group and ask them to list as many types of movement as possible for their category using the activity sheet *the five categories of movement*.

Mid-session learning stop (approx. 5 mins)

Step 1

Randomly choose a child to feed back on behalf of their group any new learning or questions from this activity.

- What have they learnt about the importance of *getting moving* so far in the lesson?

- What activities have they identified so far in their category?

- Any questions?

Step 2

Ask the remainder of the groups to reflect on their learning in a similar way. Allow the groups time to complete their lists.

Class feedback

- Ask the groups to take it in turns to mime the activities that they have identified for their category of movement.

- The remainder of the class have to guess what activity is being mimed.

- Keep a count of both the number of activities that are identified for each category and how many of these activities the remainder of the class recognises.

- Congratulate the group which comes up with the most number of activities that are recognised by the rest of the class.

Extension activity: Visualise success

Time allowing, introduce the class to the concept of visualisation as set out in this activity and suggest that pupils may wish to complete the worksheet *Visualise success*.

Take Away activity: My activity diary

Ask the class to keep an activity diary over the coming week and record how much time they spend in each of the five categories of movement.

Final plenary: reflect and review (approx. 10 mins)

- Revisit the learning objectives for the session with the class and discuss whether the learning outcomes have been met.

- Encourage the class to ask any questions that they have in relation to the session. Children who are able to communicate in writing can be encouraged to submit anonymous questions after the session by using the letter box.

- With their Talk Partners, ask the class to talk through something new that they have learnt in the session and then individually add the new learning and ideas to their Mind Map from the beginning of the session.

- End the session with *Pass the smile* or a similar closure activity. (For guidance on closure activities see page 44.)

✓

Name: _____ Date: _____

THE FIVE CATEGORIES OF MOVEMENT

1. Passive sitting

For example, TV, reading.

2. Active sitting

For example, TV, reading.

Copyright © Ruth MacConville 2017

3. Everyday movement

For example, walking, making your bed.

4. Vigorous movement

For example, on the go, jogging.

5 Aerobic movement

For example, the heart beats quickly, running, swimming.

Copyright © Ruth MacConville 2017

Name: _____ Date: _____

VISUALISE SUCCESS

Visualisation is a technique that involves creating images or pictures in your mind while you are in a state of relaxation.

- Help yourself to get moving by visualising yourself doing it.

- Visualising yourself running, swimming, cycling or doing any sport that you enjoy sends brain signals to your muscles that are the same as the signals that your brain sends when they are actually doing the sport.

- All great athletes practise visualisation. This is because it trains your brain to work more effectively and your body to respond automatically.

- Choose a sport that you would like to excel in.

- Lie on the floor and imagine yourself performing all the movements that you need for this sport. If you choose swimming, think about the temperature of the water, how it feels against your skin, the water splashing all around you and how your arms and legs are moving.

- At the end of the visualisation, imagine yourself winning the race and jumping up and down with happiness.

Copyright © Ruth MacConville 2017

Name: _____ Date: _____

MY ACTIVITY DIARY

- Keep an activity diary.

- Aim to be active for one hour every day.

In the boxes, write what the activity was and approximately how many minutes you spent doing it. At the end of each day, write in the total activity time.

	Activity 1	Activity 2	Activity 3	Activity 4	Activity 5	Total time
Monday	Time:	Time:	Time:	Time:	Time:	Time:
Tuesday	Time:	Time:	Time:	Time:	Time:	Time:
Wednesday	Time:	Time:	Time:	Time:	Time:	Time:
Thursday	Time:	Time:	Time:	Time:	Time:	Time:
Friday	Time:	Time:	Time:	Time:	Time:	Time:
Saturday	Time:	Time:	Time:	Time:	Time:	Time:
Sunday	Time:	Time:	Time:	Time:	Time:	Time:

Copyright © Ruth MacConville 2017

SESSION 8: HAVE FUN
Background notes

Play is probably the single, most effective mechanism by which children develop their resilience. Taking part in fun, engaging and pleasurable activities with others is crucial for a healthy, happy life for children and throughout life. Play is also the single most effective way that children develop their intrinsic motivation and an authentic sense of self. Through adventurous and playful activities children find out who they are, discover what they can do and gradually learn to realise they can manage without adult help.

In this session children explore the three main types of fun: relaxing fun, accommodating fun and challenging fun. Engaging in each type of fun is vital for a child's healthy development, as they encompass the range of full experiences that promote what Elizabeth Hartley-Brewer (2005) calls the six Cs: creativity, curiosity, confidence, concentration, physical co-ordination and co-operation.

Challenging fun can be tough, as it usually involves children engaging in sports or learning a new skill such as playing a musical instrument. Challenging play strengthens children's concentration, builds their physical strength and enhances their grit and persistence. The pre-established rules and procedures that are usually an essential element of challenging play also provide children with practice in conforming to non-negotiable rules.

Accommodating fun enables children to fine-tune their social skills and competencies. It can also be demanding, as it usually involves children showing empathy, and noticing and interpreting the intention and impact of others. It also involves adjusting their behaviour and being sensitive to the needs of others so that they are able to maintain the friendship over time.

Relaxing fun involves little social problem solving and does not usually require that children adapt their behaviour to others. It usually involves children developing their own interests, learning how to be self-sufficient and enjoying their own company.

Learning objectives

We are learning:

- the importance of enjoying three different sorts of fun

- how taking on a challenge can help us.

Learning outcomes

I can:

- tell you about the three sorts of fun

- recognise that activities requiring more effort can mean more fun in the long run

- understand the importance of taking on a new challenge.

Resources

Right Now activity:

- A really fun time

Extension activities:

- Are you a good sport?

- Get out of your comfort zone

Take Away activity:

- Three sorts of fun

Key vocabulary

- challenging

- accommodating

- social

- comfort zone

Pre-teaching session

Children with special educational needs and disabilities may benefit from a short pre-teaching session to introduce them to the key vocabulary that is used in this session. (For guidance on differentiation see page 62.)

Introduction (approx. 10 mins)

Open the session by reviewing the class rules that were agreed in the earlier session. Is there anything that we might like to change, amend or add before we begin the session? Remind pupils of the reasons for having rules and how they can support their learning.

- Carry out random pairing so that each child has a Talk Partner for the session. (For guidance on how to make these pairings see page 59.)

- Review the Take Away activity from the previous session.

- Write the word *fun* on the board and open the session by asking the class to suggest what this word means to them. Record their responses.

Starter activity: Draw and Write (approx. 5 mins)

Ask each child to draw a picture and write notes to record their ideas and understanding of fun.

Right Now activity: A really fun time (approx. 10 mins)

Explain that this activity lists the top 14 fun activities that were identified by researchers who talked to thousands of children about what they enjoyed most. The activities are listed in order of popularity. The most popular activity is sport, and the least popular activity is school.

Ask the children to complete the activity that involves numbering the activities according to how much fun they think they are.

Remember to emphasise the importance of personal preferences, i.e. what is great fun for one person may not be fun for somebody else; we are all different, and it is important to be ourselves.

Class discussion: Three sorts of fun (approx. 10 mins)

Explain to the class that although there are many different sorts of things that we can do to have fun, there are three main *types* or categories of fun. Ask the class to suggest what these three types of fun might be. Record their suggestions.

Introduce the three types of fun:

1. *Challenging fun* is about learning new skills: learning to play sports, for example, involves learning new skills such as how to use equipment and understanding special rules and new words. Learning a new sport takes practice and a lot of time. It can be frustrating, but slowly, playing the sport becomes great fun. Being part of a team and winning is exciting and worth all the hard work. Learning to play a musical instrument, and how to draw or paint really well, are also challenging sorts of fun.

2. *Accommodating fun* is about fitting in with others: for example, going out on a family trip to the park or zoo, going shopping with friends or organising a party. Accommodating fun is about making plans, showing up at the right time, and organising activities and celebrations with friends. It involves thinking about others and sharing happy times together.

3. *Relaxing fun* is about taking time out to do the things that we enjoy doing on our own. It is about being in our comfort zone, feeling relaxed and comfortable, and enjoying doing our own thing. This could be listening to music, screen time or reading.

Right Now activity: A really fun time continued (approx. 10 mins)

Ask the class to go through the list of activities and this time use the second column on the worksheet to label each of the activities with either *C* for challenging, *A* for accommodating or *R* for relaxing.

Mid-session learning stop (approx. 5 mins)

Step 1

Randomly choose a child so that the whole class is focused as they do not know who will be selected. Ask the child to explain:

- where they are up to with completing the task

- if they have any questions or comments

- if they need any advice or help.

Step 2

Ask the rest of the class to reflect on their work in a similar way.

Class discussion (approx. 10 mins)

Introduce the idea that the activities that make us feel really good about ourselves are sometimes the most challenging. Although they usually need a lot of energy, time and planning, in the long run they can make us feel happier and good about ourselves.

Explore with the class the idea that the more effort that we put into fun activities the more enjoyable they are in the long run.

Extension activities:

- Are you a good sport?

- Get out of your comfort zone

Take Away activity: Three sorts of fun

Introduce the class to the task of keeping a Fun diary that shows the time that they spend enjoying the three different types of fun.

Final plenary: reflect and review (approx. 10 mins)

- Revisit the learning objectives for the session with the class and discuss whether the learning outcomes have been met.

- Encourage the class to ask any questions that they have in relation to the session. Children who are able to communicate in writing can be encouraged to submit anonymous questions after the session by using the letter box.

- With their Talk Partners, ask the class to talk through what they have learnt in the session and then individually add to their Draw and Write activity on Fun using a different colour pen to show their new ideas and learning.

- End the session with *Pass the smile* or a similar closure activity. (For guidance on closure activities see page 44.)

Name: _____ Date: _____

A REALLY FUN TIME

Here are 14 activities that were voted as being the most fun by thousands of children. Read the list carefully and then choose what the most fun item is for you. Put a 1 in the box by your first choice. Then choose your second favourite fun activity and put a 2 in the box by it. Then rate all the other activities up to 14. Use the larger box to describe a really fun time.

1. Sports		8. Summer holiday	
2. Theme parks		9. Parties	
3. Games/toys		10. Shopping	
4. Friends		11. The beach	
5. Outdoor adventure		12. Cafes/restaurants	
6. Films		13. Christmas presents	
7. Travel		14. School	

Describe a really fun time

Copyright © Ruth MacConville 2017

Name: _____ Date: _____

ARE YOU A GOOD SPORT?

All team games have rules that we need to learn in order to play the game.

Write down three of these rules:

1. _____

2. _____

3. _____

There are also other rules that we need for playing team games that are not written down. Knowing these unwritten rules can help you to be a good sport.

Read the sentences below and then circle Yes or No for each one.

1.	I always accept what the referee says.	Yes	No
2.	I work harder when it looks like the other team are winning.	Yes	No
3.	I shake hands with the other team when the game is finished.	Yes	No
4.	I let my disappointment show when the other team wins.	Yes	No
5.	I remember to say 'Well done' when the other team wins.	Yes	No
6.	I just walk away after the game if my team loses.	Yes	No
7.	I argue with the referee's decisions.	Yes	No
8.	I blame my team members if we lose the game.	Yes	No
9.	I insult the other team players when they are doing well.	Yes	No
10.	I make excuses when I don't play my best.	Yes	No

Now check your answers: Give yourself a point for each right answer.

1. Yes; 2. Yes; 3. Yes; 4. No; 5. Yes; 6. No; 7. No; 8. No; 9. No; 10. No

If you scored five or more, you are a good sport. Congratulations!

If you scored less than five, look carefully again at your answers and talk to a trusted adult about how to be a better sport.

Copyright © Ruth MacConville 2017

Name: _____ Date: _____

GET OUT OF YOUR COMFORT ZONE

We all need a comfort zone, a special place where we feel safe, comfortable and relaxed. It's also important that you sometimes:

- get out of your comfort zone

- learn something new

- get better at something you already know

- help yourself to overcome a fear.

1. In the comfort zone circle below, draw or write the names of all the things that make your comfort zone a special place.

2. Promise yourself that you will get out of your comfort zone once a week or more.

3. Keep a list of all your efforts.

4. Find a friend and get out of your comfort zones together.

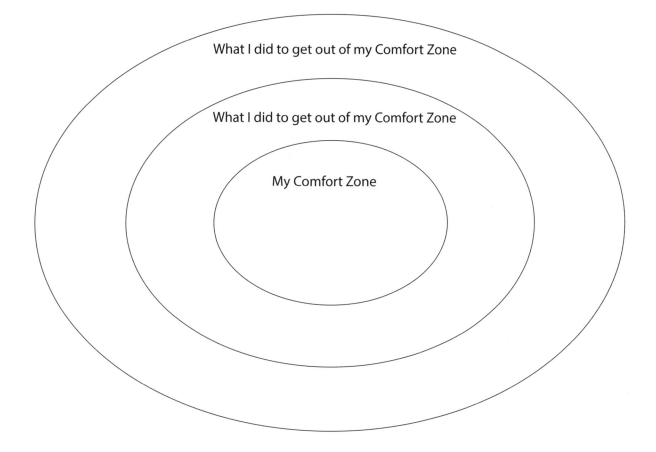

Copyright © Ruth MacConville 2017

Name: _____ Date: _____

THREE SORTS OF FUN

In the boxes below list all the fun activities that you enjoy in each category.

Challenging fun

Accommodating fun

Relaxing fun

Copyright © Ruth MacConville 2017

SESSION 9: TELEVISION TURNOFF

Background notes

The aim of this session is to enable children to become aware of the amount of time they spend watching television and using computers, iPads and smart phones. Television is the number one leisure activity in Europe and the United States, consuming, on average, more than half of our free time (Schor 2004). Although television is a way to relax for a while each day, there is increasing evidence that we are more motivated to watch our favourite shows and keep up with our favourite characters when we are feeling lonely or need social connection (Lieberman 2013). Although watching television can satisfy our social needs to some extent in the short term, it can also 'crowd out' other activities and mean that we spend less time with our friends. Countless studies have shown that we eat more when we are distracted by a screen, whether TV, tablet or computer. A study of 9–14-year-old boys showed that not only did they eat more while watching TV, but the larger quantities of food did not make them feel fuller. What was happening on the screen was more interesting to these boys than what was happening in real life (Benelam 2009). An American study reported in Schor (2004) suggested that excessive television and screen time is associated with lower cognitive skills, academic achievement and increased obesity. It can also lead to unrealistic expectations of affluence and increased materialism. The same study also suggested that most children would prefer to be out and about engaged in sports and other activities than staying at home watching TV.

Learning objectives

We are learning to:

- recognise how much time we spend watching TV or using screens

- discover what other activities we can do instead.

Learning outcomes

We are learning to:

- explore fun alternatives to watching television and using screens

- build healthy screen-time habits.

Resources

Right Now activity:

- Instead of watching TV I could…

Extension activity:

- Screen time

Take Away activity:

- My fit prime time

Key vocabulary

- statistics

Pre-teaching session

Children with special educational needs and disabilities may benefit from a short pre-teaching session to introduce them to the key vocabulary that is used in this session. (For guidance on differentiation see page 62.)

Introduction (approx. 10 mins)

- Open the session by reviewing the class rules that were agreed in the earlier session. Is there anything that we might like to change, amend or add before we begin the session? Remind pupils of the reasons for having rules and how they can support their learning.

- Carry out random pairing so that each child has a Talk Partner for the session. (For guidance on how to make these pairings see page 59.)

- Review the Take Away activitiy from the previous session.

- Write the following sentence on the board:

    Children, on average, watch at least four hours of television every day. Most of this television is watched during 'prime time', i.e. between 4pm and 9pm.

Talk Partner and group discussion (approx. 10 mins)

With their Talk Partners, ask the class to explore:

- what they think about this statistic and why

- what programmes they enjoy watching on TV

- what they could do instead of watching TV.

Ask the Talk Partners to *snowball* or join up with two other pairs and compare their answers. Randomly choose a child to feed back on behalf of their group. Repeat this process until there has been feedback from each of the groups.

Record the ideas about activities that children can do instead of watching TV.

Right Now activity: Instead of watching TV I could... (approx. 5 mins)

Ask each child to complete this activity.

Mid-session learning stop (approx. 5 mins)

Step 1

Randomly choose a child so that the whole class is focused, not knowing who will be selected. Ask the child to explain:

- where they are up to with completing the task
- if they have any questions or comments
- if they need any advice or help.

Step 2

Ask the rest of the class to reflect on their work in a similar way. Allow time for the class to complete the task.

Class discussion (approx. 10 mins): Healthy screen-time habits

Ask the class to suggest healthy screen-time habits.
Suggestions may include the following:

- choose the TV programmes that you watch carefully: don't just sit there
- only watch the programmes that you really enjoy
- if you find yourself just sitting watching television and not really enjoying it, get moving and find something to do that is more fun.

Record the children's suggestions.

Extension activity

- Screen time

Take Away activity: My fit prime time

Ask the children to keep a record over the coming week of the times that they choose not to watch television and to engage in different activities instead.

Ask the class to collect a variety of advertisements from magazines or newspapers and bring them to the next session.

Final plenary: reflect and review (approx. 10 mins)

- Revisit the learning objectives for the session with the class and discuss whether the learning outcomes have been met.
- Encourage the class to ask any questions that they have in relation to the session. Children who are able to communicate in writing can be encouraged to submit anonymous questions after the session by using the letter box.

- With their Talk Partners, ask the class to talk through and then individually complete the evaluation.

- End the session with *Pass the smile* or a similar closure activity. (For guidance on closure activities see page 44.)

Name: _____ Date: _____

INSTEAD OF WATCHING TV I COULD...

Make a list of the top ten fun things you could do instead of watching TV.

1	
2	
3	
4	
5	
6	
7	
8	
9	
10	

Now make it happen!

Copyright © Ruth MacConville 2017

Name: _____ Date: _____

SCREEN TIME

Choose a day.

Fill in the graph to show how much time you spent looking at screens.

Day: _____

Hours					
5					
4					
3					
2					
1					
	TV	Internet	Text Messaging	DVD	PC and Video Games

Copyright © Ruth MacConville 2017

Name: _____ Date: _____

MY FIT PRIME TIME

Here are the top six activities that children do instead of watching television:

1. Chat   2. Reading   3. Hobbies   4. Play   5. Help around the home   6. Exercise

Keep a diary for one week and in each box write down the things from the list that you do instead of watching TV.

	4–5pm	5–6pm	6–7pm	7–8pm	8–9pm
Monday					
Tuesday					
Wednesday					
Thursday					
Friday					
Saturday					
Sunday					

Copyright © Ruth MacConville 2017

SESSION 10: THINK TWICE

Background notes

This session introduces the concept of media literacy – the ability to understand what ideas and products advertisements are trying to sell us, and most importantly *how* they are doing this. Numerous companies spend millions of pounds each year on clever adverts to attract children to their products so that they will use what advertisers call 'pester power' to pressure their parents to buy the products. Studies suggest that although as children become older they become less trusting of adverts, they remain extremely vulnerable to the advertisers' persuasive powers. Media psychologists Daniel Acuff and Robert Reiher (2005) explain that this is because adverts are carefully designed to manipulate children's attention and 'downshift' the brain, i.e. bypass the neo-cortex – the 'thinking brain' – and activate the emotional midbrain and its instinctive reactive centres. 'Downshifting' makes it virtually impossible for children to think critically, or even think at all, while watching adverts. Acuff and Reiher suggest that it takes effective media literacy training to develop children's critical reasoning and thus ensure that they are less vulnerable to the advertisers' emotional ploys.

Learning objectives

We are learning to:

- understand that advertisers are there to make us want to buy their products

- understand some of the ways that advertisers do this.

Learning outcomes

I can:

- identify the messages that advertisements and other media messages want to get across

- work out *how* advertisers make us want to buy their products.

Resources

A selection of magazines and newspaper advertisements.

Right Now activities:

- What's going on?

- The Children's Manifesto

Extension activities:

- Shop smart

- Let's go shopping

Take Away activities:

- My favourite advert
- Media messages

Key vocabulary

- product
- advertisement
- influence
- design
- downshifting

Pre-teaching session

Children with special educational needs and disabilities may benefit from a short pre-teaching session to introduce them to the key vocabulary that is used in this session. (For guidance on differentiation see page 62.)

Introduction (approx. 10 mins)

- Open the session by reviewing the class rules that were agreed in the earlier session. Is there anything that we might like to change, amend or add before we begin the session? Remind the class of the reasons for having rules and how they can support their learning.

- Carry out random pairing so that each child has a Talk Partner for the session (see page 59 for guidance on how to make these pairings).

- Review the Take Away activity from the previous session.

- Write the following sentence on the board:

    Adverts are all around us. They have been designed to influence how we feel so that we really want to buy what they are selling.

- With their Talk Partners, ask the class to discuss whether they agree or disagree with this statement. Take feedback on the discussion and take a tally on how many agree/disagree with the statement.

Starter activity: Draw and Write: Adverts (approx. 5 mins)

Each child is to complete a Draw and Write activity on *Adverts*. (For guidance on using Draw and Write activities see page 41.)

Class discussion (approx. 10 mins)

Lead a class discussion on the following points:

- The purpose of adverts is to sell us something, and they sometimes do this by making us feel that there is something wrong with us.

- Adverts promise us that buying their product will make us look better, have more fun or have more friends.

- How many times have you seen an advert only to feel that you immediately have to go shopping and buy the product or ask an adult to buy it for you?

- The problem is that most of the promises that the adverts make are not true.

Talk Partner discussion: Good buy, bad buy? (approx. 5 mins)

With their Talk Partners, ask the class to think about the last time they bought something new or asked an adult to buy it for them because they saw it on an advert: you couldn't wait to use it, play with it or wear it, but how long were you happy with the new purchase or were you disappointed very quickly?

Randomly choose a child to feed back on this discussion.

Group activity (approx. 10 mins)

With their Talk Partners, ask the class to *snowball* or join up to make groups of six children. Ask each group to select an advert and answer the following questions:

- What is the advert trying to sell us?

- How is it doing this?

- Does the picture help to get the advertiser's message across?

- How did the advert make us feel?

Take feedback from the groups and encourage a class discussion, asking the class to explore the pressure that they may feel to buy what they see in the adverts.

If time allows, ask the groups to repeat this activity using another advert, and take feedback.

Class discussion (approx. 10 mins)

Explain to the class that although we all know that adverts are there to persuade us to buy things, advertisers do this in very clever ways. Most adverts are designed to bypass the thinking part of our brain and work on our feelings.

Talk Partner discussion (approx. 5 mins)

With their Talk Partners, ask the class to think about how they *feel* when they watch advertisements. Randomly choose a child to feed back on this discussion.

Class discussion continued

One of the ways that advertisers influence us is by what they call 'downshifting', which means turning off the thinking part of our brain and turning on our feelings instead. Advertisements are designed to make us *feel*, not *think*.

Advertisers sell us an idea that goes along with their product:

- If you buy this product you will *feel* happy, cool, fit, popular, grown up, successful.

- If you don't buy this product you will *feel* left out, uncool, unfit.

Right Now activity: What's going on? (approx. 10 mins)

Distribute a copy of the activity sheet *What's going on?* to each child. With their Talk Partners, ask the class to take it in turns to describe their favourite advert and then talk through the questions together. Then each child completes the activity sheet individually, each describing their own favourite advert.

Mid-session learning stop (approx. 5 mins)

Step 1

Randomly choose a child to feed back on this activity. Ask the child to explain:

- where they are up to with completing the task

- if they have any questions or comments

- if they need any advice or help.

Step 2

Ask the rest of the class to reflect on their work in a similar way. Allow the class time to complete the task.

Right Now activity: The Children's Manifesto (approx. 10 mins)

- Distribute copies of the Manifesto and, with their Talk Partners, ask the class to complete the activity, which involves selecting agree or disagree for each of the items listed in the Manifesto.

- Read out each sentence and ask each child to put up their hand if they agree with the sentence that they have just heard. Take a tally on the number of children who agree with the sentence, then ask each child to put up their hand if they disagree with the sentence and take another tally. After all the sentences have been read out, share the overall scores with the class.

- Allow time for the class to discuss some of the issues raised if they want to.

Extension activities

- Shop smart
- Let's go shopping

Take Away activity: My favourite advert

Introduce and explain the worksheet *My favourite advert.*

Take Away activity: Media messages

Introduce and explain the worksheet *Media messages.*

Final plenary: reflect and review (approx. 10 mins)

- Revisit the learning objectives for the session with the class and discuss whether the learning outcomes have been met.

- Encourage the class to ask any questions that they have in relation to the session. Children who are able to communicate in writing can be encouraged to submit anonymous questions after the session by using the letter box.

- With their Talk Partners, ask the class to talk through what they have learnt in the session and then individually add new ideas and learning using a different colour pen to the Draw and Write activity on Adverts from the beginning of the session.

- End the session with *Pass the smile* or a similar closure activity. (For guidance on closure activities see page 44.)

Name: _____ Date: _____

WHAT'S GOING ON?

Choose one of your favourite adverts and then answer the questions.

1. What is the advert trying to sell you?

2. How is the advert doing this?

3. Lots of adverts on the TV or in films tell a little story. Is there a story in the advert that you have chosen?

Copyright © Ruth MacConville 2017

4. How does this advert make you feel?

5. How is the advert trying to make you buy the product?

6. What is the key message in this advert?

Copyright © Ruth MacConville 2017

Name: _____ Date: _____

THE CHILDREN'S MANIFESTO

	Agree	Disagree
Please be honest with us about your products.		
Please treat us with respect.		
Please take us seriously.		
Please stop advertising products that are bad for us.		
Don't tell us that *all* food is healthy, because it isn't.		
Don't pressure us into buying things.		
Don't encourage us to pester our parents to buy us things.		
Don't tell us that our parents and teachers aren't cool.		
Don't make us feel bad for not buying stuff.		
Leave our friendships alone.		
Don't promise us we will be happy if we buy your stuff.		
Tell us if a game or a website is not suitable for us.		
Set up children's panels so that we can tell you what we think.		
Tell us how much you spend on advertising to children every year.		
Is there anything else that you would like to say? Write it in the box below.		

(Adapted from Mayo and Nairn 2009)

Copyright © Ruth MacConville 2017

Name: _____ Date: _____

SHOP SMART

You've saved up all your pocket money and birthday money and you are in the shop with a new toy in your hand. You are walking towards the cash register – you know the toy is useless and that you are going to be sorry that you bought it, but you still really want it…

You need to stop and ask yourself the following questions:

(Answer Yes or No to each one)

1. Do I really need this? _____

2. Do I know what I am going to do with it? _____

3. Would my best friend tell me to spend my savings on this toy? _____

4. Will I still like this toy in a few months' time? _____

5. I have made some bad buys before – will this toy be another one? _____

6. Could I live without this toy? _____

7. I'm saving up for something big, so do I really want to spend my savings on this toy? _____

If your answers were mostly **Yes**, buy the toy, but remember to ask for a receipt, so that if you do change your mind you can take it back to the shop later on.

If your answers were mainly **No**:

· Put the toy down.

· Walk out of the shop.

· You will feel happy as you walk away.

Copyright © Ruth MacConville 2017

Name: _____ Date: _____

LET'S GO SHOPPING

Most children enjoy going shopping with their friends. Have you ever thought what makes it so exciting?

Remember the last time you went to the shopping centre and then circle True or False for the following sentences:

You're happy because you are with your friend and you have money to spend.	True	False
You enjoy the bright lights, listening to the music and smelling the pizza.	True	False
You look at the shop window displays and the adverts but you forget that there are no windows to the outside world.	True	False
By the cash register there are lots of cheap things to buy.	True	False
You decide to buy some of these small things as you stand in the queue waiting to pay.	True	False

If you answered True to these questions, these are the things that shop owners do to make you enjoy shopping. Notice them next time you go to a shopping centre.

Now think of some other things that make shopping exciting for you.

Copyright © Ruth MacConville 2017

Name: _____ Date: _____

MY FAVOURITE ADVERT

Write about your favourite advertisement.

Where did you see the advertisement?

What was it for?

What was it selling?

Does the advert tell a little story? Tell this story in a few words.

Did you want to buy it?

Did you buy it?

What happened next?

Copyright © Ruth MacConville 2017

Name: _____ Date: _____

MEDIA MESSAGES

Make a list of ten media messages that you receive during the week. Say where the message came from. Think about how it made you feel.

Media message	From	How did it make you feel?
1.		
2.		
3.		
4.		
5.		
6.		
7.		
8.		
9.		
10.		

Copyright © Ruth MacConville 2017

SESSION 11: PICTURES, PICTURES EVERYWHERE!

Background notes

This session explores how advertisers create images of beautiful people by blurring the boundaries between fiction and reality. Carefully manipulated and computer-merged images of the best features of several models are presented as being one real person. Discussion and activities will explore some examples of these images and the amount of work, i.e. digital manipulation, that goes into making them. Children continuously see images of beautiful people in the media and many feel that this is what they should aspire to look like. This is because advertisers try to convince us that being the 'wrong' size or not having the 'perfect' body is bad for us. They do this by promising us that if we buy their product we will look like the model in the picture. One of the ways that we can encourage children to be realistic about their appearance is to enable them to look critically at media images and recognise the difference between a *real* person and a computer-generated image.

Learning objectives

We are learning to:

- understand that most photographs in adverts are there to promote the *right* appearance

- recognise that many images of the models that we see in the media are computer-generated

- understand that media images are designed to make us feel that we need to buy the products that adverts are promoting.

Learning outcomes

I can:

- look carefully at adverts of models and understand that they probably don't look like that in real life

- tell you why advertisers make the models look much better than they do in real life.

Resources

Dove Evolution – with some images all is not what it seems (available on YouTube).

A selection of advertisements and photographs that have been digitally altered.

Right Now activity:

- Think real: positive thinking habits

Take Away activity:

- Get dressed

Key vocabulary

- digital manipulation
- images
- airbrushing
- enhanced
- media

Pre-teaching session

Children with special educational needs and disabilities may benefit from a short pre-teaching to introduce them to the key vocabulary that is used in this session. (For guidance on differentiation see page 62.)

Introduction (approx. 10 mins)

- Open the session by reviewing the class rules that were agreed in the earlier session. Is there anything that we might like to change, amend or add before we begin the session? Remind pupils of the reasons for having rules and how they can support their learning.

- Carry out random pairing so that each child has a Talk Partner for the session (see page 59 for guidance on how to make these pairings).

- Review the Take Away activities from the previous session.

- Write the following statement on the board:

    Most images that we see in adverts and on television are fake.

- With their Talk Partners, ask the class whether this statement is true or false. Explore the reasons for their answers.

- Take a tally on how many children think that this is true and how many think that it is false.

- Ask the class to suggest reasons for their decision.

Starter activity: Draw and Write activity: A Photoshopped model

Ask the children to choose a photo of a model from a magazine and label it with suggestions of how the picture has been manipulated. Add a few sentences explaining why advertisers make these changes. (For guidance on Draw and Write activities see page 41.)

Show a video clip that demonstrates how the media can change an individual's appearance through manipulating (i.e. changing) a photograph, for example Dove Evolution on YouTube.

Class discussion (approx. 15 mins)

Explain that most of the models we see in magazines, films, adverts, newspapers and on TV and the internet have been changed so much that they no longer look anything like they do in real life. Even the models themselves don't recognise their images in the adverts.

Ask the class to comment on these issues and encourage them to consider the feelings and thoughts of the models involved.

Talk Partner discussion

Choose an advertisement from a magazine or newspaper and, with their Talk Partners, ask the class to answer the following questions as a basis for discussion:

- What do they see?

- What do the models in the advert look like?

- Are they for real?

- How do they think the advertisers are trying to make us feel?

- Why are they doing this?

- Will buying the product make us look like the model in the picture?

Class discussion continued

Adverts showing very beautiful models are all around us; however, hardly anybody in real life looks like the models in the advert (not even the models themselves). Do you think that you should try to look like the models that are shown in the media?

Although hardly any people look like the models that we see in the adverts, advertisers still use them to make the rest of us feel that we should look like them. They want us to believe that if we buy their products we will look like the models in the advertisements. How do advertisers do this?

Media messages are enhanced: this means that special effects are used to make models look better than they do in real life. Ask for suggestions from the class of what these special effects might be and how they work.

Digital alteration techniques include the following:

- Airbrushing: this makes models look perfect by lightening, darkening or smoothing out their skin and covering up imperfections such as spots, moles and bruises.

- Digital enhancement: this makes models look perfect by changing their body shapes. It can make legs longer, flatten stomachs, smooth bumps and change the shape of their facial features (nose, mouth, eyes). It can also make a model's hair appear more shiny and thick, their teeth look whiter and change the colour of their eyes.

- Digital manipulation: this makes models look thinner and taller, and their shoulders look broader. Photo editors take the best parts of two models and then put them together to make one perfect model. Films do this too. They use one model's legs, another model's hands and a third model's face. In the end, not even the models look like themselves in the photos.

Explain to the class that when models are Photoshopped it creates an image or picture that is not real. It is too perfect. It is important to remember that nobody, not even the models themselves, look as good as they do in the adverts. It is therefore important not to compare yourself with the models that you see in the advertisements. Models can feel unhappy when they see how they look in the adverts.

Advertisers spend a huge amount of money to make you feel that you can't do without their product. They want you to believe that you need their product to look good, be happy, be loved, have lots of friends and be successful. Becoming more mindful and thinking really carefully about how the adverts work will help you to realise that the models you see in the adverts are not real and buying the products won't make you look like them.

Right Now activity: Think real: positive thinking habits (approx. 5 mins)

Explain the activity to the class:

Read each of the ten sentences carefully and at the end of each one think to yourself 'Is this true of me or not?' Let's do the first one together: read the sentence carefully, and if you think that you will compare yourself to the models you see in the adverts, choose 'True' and write it on the little line at the end of the sentence. If you think that this is not true for you and that you won't compare yourself to the models, choose 'False'. Read the rest of the sentences, think carefully about whether each one is true or false for you, and write down your answer. When you have completed this work, count up your answers. How many were 'True' and how many were 'False'?

Mid-session learning stop (approx. 5 mins)

Step 1

Randomly choose a child to feed back on this activity. Ask the child to explain:

- where they are up to with completing the task

- if they have any questions or comments

- if they need any advice or help.

Step 2

Ask the rest of the class to reflect on their work in a similar way. Allow the class time to complete the task.

Extension activity

One of the most successful adverts ever showed a glass holding a toothbrush with the words 'Twice a day'. Ask the children to each design an advert that has a very short, healthy message.

Take Away activity: Get dressed

Explain the activity to the class:

> This activity is based on the book *Get Dressed* by the designer and illustrator Seymour Chaste. In this book, Seymour celebrates the daily routine of getting dressed and the individuality of all our choices. Do you get dressed to hide? To read about dragons? Seymour teaches us that there is a lot more to getting dressed than just thinking about how we look. Read the sentences carefully and think about all the different reasons that you get dressed.

Final plenary: reflect and review (approx. 10 mins)

- Revisit the learning outcomes for the session with the class and discuss whether the learning objectives for the session have been met.

- Encourage the class to ask any questions that they have in relation to the session. Children who are able to communicate in writing can be encouraged to submit anonymous questions after the session by using the question box.

- Distribute a copy of the evaluation *What have I learnt?* to each child.

- With their Talk Partners, ask the class to talk through and then individually complete the evaluation.

- End the session with *Pass the smile* or a similar closure activity. (For guidance on closure activities see page 44.)

Name: _____   Date: _____

THINK REAL: POSITIVE THINKING HABITS

Positive thinking habits can stop us comparing ourselves to the models we see in the adverts. Read the sentences below and write True or False for each one.

- I won't compare myself to models in the adverts. _____

- If I see an advertisement that makes me want to change something about myself and feel down, I will remember that this is all part of the advertiser's clever plan to make me buy their product. _____

- Advertisers use the pictures of the models to persuade me that if I buy their product I will look like the model in the advert. _____

- I will remember that even the models sometimes do not recognise themselves in the adverts. _____

- I will remember that how most models look in the adverts is not real. _____

- I can learn to enjoy looking at pictures of beautiful people without feeling unhappy about myself. _____

- Appearance is an important part of me and I care about how I look, but what matters most is who I am and what I can do. _____

- The people I love do not look like the models in the advertisements. _____

- My friends do not look like the models in the advertisements. _____

- The people I see all around me at home, in school, at the shops and in the park do not look like the models in the advertisements. _____

Count your answers: How many True? _____ How many False? _____

If you got more than six for True, well done.

If you got less than six, talk to a trusted adult about your answers.

Copyright © Ruth MacConville 2017

Name: _____   Date: _____

GET DRESSED

There is a lot more to getting dressed than just how you look.

Read the reasons below and then answer Yes or No to each one.

Then add some ideas of your own in the empty boxes.

I dress:	Yes/No	I dress:	Yes/No
To keep dry		For breakfast	
To keep warm		To have pockets	
To keep cool		To please my family	
To look cool		To please my teacher	
To look taller		To please myself	
For work		To go to a party	
For play		To be comfortable	
For school		To look like somebody else	
For sleep		To look stylish	
For sports		To disguise myself	
For dinner		To cover things up	

SESSION 12: THOUGHT CATCHING

Background notes

The purpose of this session is to introduce the basic teachings of cognitive behaviour therapy (CBT) – the fact that our thoughts, feelings and behaviours are all connected. CBT focuses on the present rather than on the past and shows us that reframing, i.e. making a change to the way that we think, can help us to manage our feelings and our behaviours. Children and young people sometimes experience anxious and negative thoughts. These thoughts often reinforce a lack of confidence and low levels of self-esteem. With practice, children can learn to 'catch' these negative thoughts and reframe them, i.e. replace them with more positive thoughts. Positive thoughts enable children to be more in control and to change their behaviour. The purpose of this session is to introduce the skills devised by Seligman (1995) that enable children to identify and manage their negative automatic thoughts (NATs) and replace them with positive automatic thoughts (PATs).

Four key skills

Seligman (1995) explains that there are four key skills involved in managing our negative automatic thoughts and restructuring our thinking:

1. The first step is to 'catch' the negative automatic thoughts (NATs) that come into our minds.

2. The second skill is recognising that what these NATs are telling us may not be true.

3. The third skill is to stop ourselves from thinking the worst.

4. The fourth skill is about generating more accurate explanations.

Throughout this session it is important to remind the class that the examples they use should not be based on their own experience. (For further guidance on using distancing techniques see page 51 of this resource.)

Learning objectives

We are learning to:

- recognise our negative thoughts

- replace them with positive thoughts

- understand that there are different types of negative thoughts.

Learning outcomes

I can:

- 'catch' my negative thoughts

- think to myself: is this thought true?

- reframe or change my negative thought into a more realistic and positive thought.

Resources

Right Now activity:

- Catch that thought

Extension activity:

- Tricky situations

Take Away activity:

- Storm in a teacup

Key vocabulary

- negative automatic thought (NAT)

- positive automatic thought (PAT)

- survive

- reframe

Pre-teaching session

Children with special educational needs and disabilities may benefit from a short pre-teaching session to introduce them to the key vocabulary that is used in this session. (For guidance on differentiation see page 62.)

Introduction (approx. 10 mins)

- Open the session by reviewing the class rules that were agreed in the earlier session. Is there anything that we might like to change, amend or add before we begin the session? Remind pupils of the reasons for having rules and how they can support their learning.

- Carry out random pairing so that each child has a Talk Partner for the session (for guidance on random pairings see page 59).

- Review the Take Away activity from the previous session.

Note: Throughout the session it is important to remind the class to not use examples of negative thinking from their own experience. (For guidance on using distancing techniques see page 51 of this resource.)

In this session we are going to start to think about our thoughts and the sorts of things that they can tell us in different situations. Sometimes negative automatic thoughts (NATs) pop into our head and tell us:

- things about ourselves that are not true: I'm not very good at sports

- things about other people: I don't think Sam will invite me to his birthday party

- what might happen in the future: I'm not going to do well in the maths test.

Learning to 'catch' these NATs is important because they can:

- make us feel down

- take away our confidence

- stop us doing our best or making new friends.

The best thing we can do when we catch a NAT is to stop and say something kind to ourselves.

Right Now activity: Catch that thought (approx. 10 mins)

With their Talk Partners, ask the class to think about the following situations and sorts of NATs that the children might say to themselves:

- On Friday it was Sam's turn to give the class a talk. He thought to himself:

  ....

  ....

- Tom was getting ready for a maths test. He said to himself:

  ....

  ....

- Rosie was getting ready to go away on a school trip. She had never been away by herself before. She said to herself:

  ....

  ....

Now make up another example using the *Catch that thought* triangle:

....

....

Take feedback on this activity.

Class discussion (approx. 10 mins)

It is easy for us to have NATs because scientists have discovered that we all have a 'negative bias' – a tendency to quickly spot things that might go wrong. A long time ago being able to do this was very helpful because life was dangerous and looking out and spotting dangers such as a tiger jumping out of the bushes helped people to survive. Today our lives are not dangerous so we do not have to be on the lookout for danger all the time. However, our brains have not caught up with this and so we still have a 'negative bias'.

Everybody has negative thoughts, but it is important that we learn how to control them. When we are upset, sad or disappointed about something, our NATs can get out of control, but it is important to remember:

- just because you don't get invited to one party doesn't mean that you won't get invited to other parties

- just because you didn't pass the test doesn't mean that you are not going to pass the next test.

When you are angry, disappointed or sad, it is important to remember that the voice in your head might not be telling you the truth and can make you feel a whole lot worse.

Talk Partner discussion (approx. 5 mins)

With their Talk Partners, ask the class to think again about the previous three examples and choose positive things that the children could say to each other in the three situations. Choose a child to feed back on this activity, and scribe their examples. Ask the rest of the class for further examples.

Class discussion (approx. 10 mins)

Making sure that you are in control of your NATs can help you to feel happier and in control. Here's how to do it:

- Catch that negative thought as soon as it comes into your head. Hit the off button and stop it. Sometimes it can help to have something to remind you to do this, like wearing an elastic band or a friendship bracelet on your wrist and snapping it as soon as you notice a negative thought come into your head. Then do something that will help you relax, such as listening to music or texting a friend.

- Stand up to your NATs. If you wouldn't say it to your best friend, don't say it to yourself either.

- Catch the negative thought and change it into a PAT (a positive automatic thought); think to yourself *everything is fine* and carry on as usual.

Mid-session learning stop (approx. 5 mins)

Step 1

Randomly choose a child to feed back on this activity.

Step 2

Ask the rest of the class to review their work in a similar way.

Class discussion continued (approx. 5 mins)

Other ways to manage NATs include the following:

- If you can't think of something kind to say to yourself, just say 'shhhh' to yourself, which means be quiet.

- Pretend that you have a volume control in your head and turn the volume of your negative thoughts down so low that you can hardly hear them.

Extension activity

- Tricky situations

Take Away activity: Storm in a teacup

Introduce and explain the worksheet *Storm in a teacup*.

Final plenary: reflect and review (approx. 10 mins)

- Revisit the learning objectives for the session with the class and discuss whether the learning outcomes have been met.

- Encourage the class to ask any questions that they have in relation to the session. Children who are able to communicate in writing can be encouraged to submit anonymous questions after the session by using the question box.

- Review the learning of the class with a closing round asking each child to finish the sentence: *Something that I have learned that I did not know before...* The children's responses can be recorded by the teacher or a teaching assistant, or written down by the children themselves.

- End the session with *Pass the smile* or a similar closure activity. (For guidance on closure activities see page 44.)

Name: _____ Date: _____

CATCH THAT THOUGHT

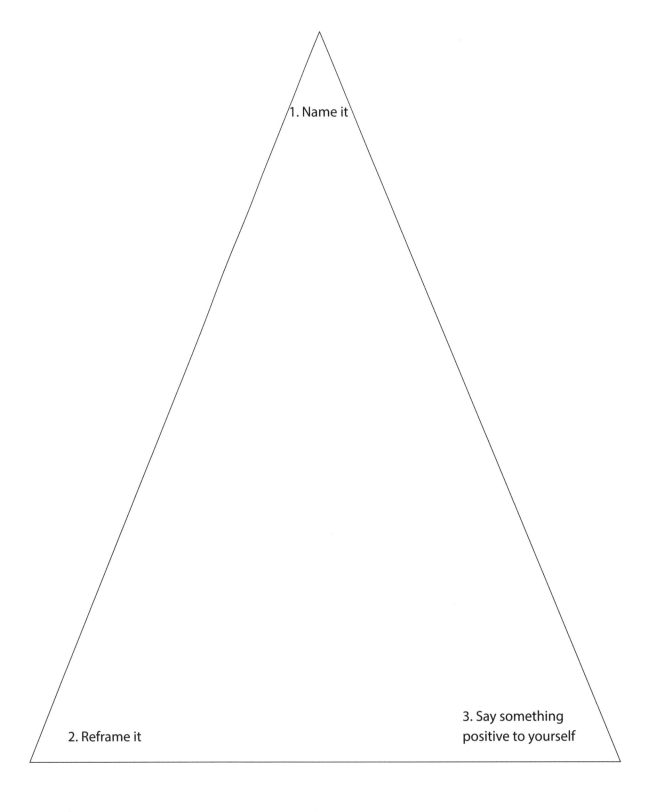

1. Name it

2. Reframe it

3. Say something positive to yourself

Copyright © Ruth MacConville 2017

Name: _____ Date: _____

TRICKY SITUATIONS

Here is a list of the top six thinking errors:

1. Binocular vision: thinking about things in a way that makes them appear bigger or smaller than they really are.

2. Black-and-white thinking: thinking about things as being all good or all bad, never or always, or all or nothing.

3. Glass half empty: only thinking about the negative parts of things.

4. Fortune telling: saying what will happen in the future without any evidence for it.

5. Taking the blame: blaming yourself for things that aren't your fault.

6. Blaming others: blaming others for things that you should take responsibility for.
   - Read the sentences below and spot the thinking errors.
   - Write the thinking error at the end of each sentence.

1. Javed's football coach gave him a lot of praise in football practice. As Javed was leaving, the coach said that Javed should practise at home. Javed *was very upset about how he had played* at the practice session.
   Thinking error: _____
   _____
   _____
   _____
   _____
   _____

2. Zulieka got a low mark on her spelling test. Now she thinks that she is the *worst pupil in the whole school.*
   Thinking error: _____
   _____
   _____
   _____
   _____
   _____

Copyright © Ruth MacConville 2017

3. Alka could not go to the park with her friends because she didn't do her homework. She thought to herself, 'I am *always* the lazy one. My sister is *always* the good one'.
    Thinking error: _____
    _____
    _____
    _____
    _____

4. Vina's parents are getting divorced. She thinks that *it is all her fault* because she has been doing really badly at school.
    Thinking error: _____
    _____
    _____
    _____
    _____

5. Kavita took the family dog out for a walk in the park. Her brother came along and Kavita asked him to look after the dog while she went to buy an ice cream. While she was gone Kavita's brother let the dog run away. Kavita got into big trouble for losing the dog. She *thought that her brother should get into trouble.*
    Thinking error: _____
    _____
    _____
    _____
    _____

6. Mel's teacher suggested that she should enter an art competition. Mel said she decided not to because *she knew that she would not win* the art competition.
    Thinking error: _____
    _____
    _____
    _____
    _____

Copyright © Ruth MacConville 2017

Name: _____ Date: _____

STORM IN A TEACUP

- Draw a picture of an imaginary character and their problem in the teacup.

- In the speech bubbles write down the things that the person could say to make themselves feel better.

Copyright © Ruth MacConville 2017

SESSION 13: MY ABC
Background notes

The purpose of this session is to give children further practice using the skills of cognitive behaviour therapy (CBT) to enable them to successfully manage challenging situations and learn how to reframe their thoughts and responses to be more flexible. Regularly reframing our thoughts and responses can create new neural pathways so that, over time, positive thinking becomes a habit.

CBT shows us that how we feel does not just come out of the blue, and although it is tempting to believe that feeling bad is triggered by a negative event, CBT teaches us that it is not what happens to us that determines how we feel but rather *what we think* about what has happened to us. It does this by first breaking the problem into smaller parts following a process of ABC.

- A stands for action (the activating event). This is often referred to as the trigger, i.e. the event that causes us to have a negative thought.

- B represents the beliefs, i.e. the meaning that individuals attach to the event or trigger.

- C is the consequences, i.e. the feelings and behaviours – how we feel and what we do about what has happened.

Learning objectives

We are learning to:

- understand that our thoughts, our feelings and our behaviour are all connected

- recognise that changing our thoughts can change how we feel.

Learning outcomes

I can:

- understand that it is our thoughts, not what happens to us, that trigger how we feel

- make positive thinking become a habit.

Resources

Right Now activity:

- My ABC

Take Away activity:

- More ABC

Key vocabulary

- negative
- positive
- influence
- reframe

Pre-teaching session

Children with special educational needs and disabilities may benefit from a short pre-teaching session to introduce them to the key vocabulary that is used in this session. (For guidance on differentiation see page 62.)

Introduction (approx. 10 mins)

- Open the session by reviewing the class rules that were agreed in the earlier session. Is there anything that we might like to change, amend or add before we begin the session? Remind pupils of the reasons for having rules and how they can support their learning.

- Carry out random pairing so that each child has a Talk Partner for the session (see page 59 for guidance on how to make these pairings).

- Review the Take Away activity from the previous session.

In this session we are going to explore that it is our thoughts about what happens to us that trigger how we feel rather than what actually happens to us. Something happens, we think about it, and what we think triggers how we feel. Feelings don't just suddenly come from nowhere – there is usually a thought that triggers them.

When we are very young we think about how we look in terms of facts: our hair colour, the colour of our eyes or our skin, how tall or how short we are. As we get older we meet many new people and lots of different things happen to us. All these experiences can influence how we think and feel about ourselves and our appearance, and we learn to feel positively or negatively about how we look.

If our thoughts about our appearance are realistic (based on how we really look) and if we accept our body just as it is, our body image will be positive and healthy.

We can help ourselves to keep a positive body image by using a way of thinking called ABC when things happen to us that challenge our positive feelings:

- Action: Something happens.

- Belief: What did I think about it?

- Consequences: How did I feel?

For example, if a girl passes an advertisement which shows a very beautiful model, she can either think to herself 'I wish I was beautiful like that' and feel upset, or she can think to herself 'The girl in the advert is not real and I like myself just the way I am.'

If a boy watches a film which stars a young man who is very fit and muscular, he can either think to himself 'I really wish I looked like that' and feel miserable, or he can think 'I like the way I am' and feel OK.

Right Now activity: My ABC (approx. 10 mins)

With their Talk Partners, ask the class to each make up an ABC situation until each child is clear about the process. Each child then completes the My ABC activity.

It is important to remind the class that the situations that they describe should not be based on their own experiences. (For guidance on using distancing techniques to enable children to avoid personalising issues see page 51.)

Mid-session learning stop (approx. 5 mins)

Step 1

Randomly choose a child to feed back on this activity and share their ABC example. Ask for feedback from the rest of the class on the following:

- whether the child is on the right lines

- positive points about the work

- suggestions for how the example could be improved.

Step 2

Ask the rest of the class to review their work in a similar way. Allow time for the class to finish the activity.

Take Away activity: More ABC

- Ask the children to devise another ABC scenario.

- Remind the class that their examples should not be based on their own experience.

Final plenary: reflect and review (approx. 10 mins)

- Revisit the learning objectives for the session with the class and discuss whether the learning outcomes have been met.

- Encourage the class to ask any questions that they have in relation to the session. Children who are able to communicate in writing can be encouraged to submit anonymous questions after the session by using the letter box.

- Review the learning of the class with a closing round asking each child to finish the sentence: *Something that I have learned that I did not know before…* The children's responses can be recorded by the teacher or a teaching assistant, or written down by the children themselves.

- End the session with *Pass the smile* or a similar closure activity. (For guidance on closure activities see page 44.)

Name: _____ Date: _____

MY ABC

Describe an imaginary ABC situation using the three boxes below:

A

Action: Something happens

B

Belief: What did the person think about it?

C

Consequence: How did the person feel?

Copyright © Ruth MacConville 2017

✓

Name: _____ Date: _____

MORE ABC

Describe an imaginary ABC situation using the three boxes below:

A

Action: Something happens

B

Belief: What did the person think about it?

C

Consequence: How did the person feel?

Copyright © Ruth MacConville 2017

SESSION 14: HOW TO BE A FRIEND
Background notes

Studies emphasise compelling evidence for the crucial link between successful peer relationships and children's well-being and resilience. In his book *Social: Why Our Brains are Wired to Connect*, psychologist Matthew Lieberman (2013) explains that everything we have learnt about the social brain tells us that we are wired to make and keep social connections and that we feel actual physical pain when these connections are threatened or broken. This is because our identity and sense of self are inextricably tied up with the groups that we are a part of. Increasing the social connections in our lives, then, is the most reliable way of increasing our well-being and our resilience. According to Asher, Parker and Walker (1996), children need to:

- possess the skills and attitudes necessary to be thought of as fun, resourceful and enjoyable companions

- recognise and respect the 'spirit of equality' that is at the heart of friendship

- possess skills for appropriate self-disclosure

- express caring, concern, admiration and affection in appropriate ways

- help their friends when their friends are in need

- be reliable partners

- be able to manage disagreements and prevent more serious conflicts

- be able to forgive.

Practitioners have a key role to play in promoting these key social behaviours and ensuring that schools are characterised by positive and caring interpersonal connections. Shelly Gable and colleagues (2004) have identified that showing that we are happy for another person when they share with us their good news and successes is an essential skill for building positive social connections. This session provides an opportunity for children to explore what makes a friend and encourages them to practise the key skills of friendship in their daily lives.

Learning objectives

We are learning to:

- understand what makes a good friend

- know the skills we need to be a good friend.

Learning outcomes

I can:

- tell you about the key skills of friendship

- practise the key friendship skills.

Resources

Right Now activities:

- What makes a good friend?

- It's good news

Take Away activity:

- It's how you say it

Key vocabulary

- qualities

- forgive

Pre-teaching session

Children with special educational needs and disabilities may benefit from a short pre-teaching session to introduce them to the key vocabulary that is used in this session. (For guidance on differentiation see page 62.)

Introduction (approx. 10 mins)

- Open the session by reviewing the class rules that were agreed in the earlier session. Is there anything that we might like to change, amend or add before we begin the session? Remind pupils of the reasons for having rules and how they can support their learning.

- Carry out random pairing so that each child has a Talk Partner for the session. (For guidance on how to make these pairings see page 59.)

- Review the Take Away activity from the previous session.

- Write the following sentence on the board:

  We all need a good friend.

- With their Talk Partners, ask the class whether they agree or disagree with this statement.

- Take a count on how many children agree/disagree and discuss their reasons as a class.

- Record their responses.

Starter activity: Draw and Write activity: What makes a good friend?

Ask the class to draw and write a picture illustrating the theme 'What makes a good friend?'

Right Now activity: What makes a good friend?

This short quiz assesses the quality of children's current friendships.

Children who score more than five negative responses could be at risk of being neglected or even rejected by their peers and may benefit from specific interventions to improve their social competence and understanding of friendship.

Class discussion (approx. 10 mins)

Explain that one of the most important skills to help us to get along with others is being happy for someone and listening carefully to them when they share their good news with us. Listening carefully to their news and showing that you are happy for them makes the other person feel cared for and even happier than they were before, because now they have also really enjoyed sharing their good news with you.

Right Now activity: It's good news (approx. 10 mins)

This activity involves children with their Talk Partners taking it in turns to listen to each other and then rating their Talk Partner on how well they felt listened to when they were sharing their good news.

Mid-session learning stop (approx. 5 mins)

Step 1

Randomly choose a set of Talk Partners to feed back where they are up to on this activity and how they are finding it. Ask the Talk Partners to describe anything new that they have learnt about making friends in the session so far.

Step 2

Ask the remainder of the class to review the activity in a similar way. Take feedback and allow time for children to complete the task.

Take Away activity: It's how you say it

Talk through the activity with the class.

Final plenary: reflect and review (approx. 10 mins)

- Revisit the learning objectives for the session with the class and discuss whether the learning outcomes for the session have been met.

- Encourage the class to ask any questions that they have in relation to the session. Children who are able to communicate in writing can be encouraged to submit anonymous questions after the session by using the letter box.

- With their Talk Partners, ask the class to talk through what they have learnt in the session and then individually add new ideas and learning using a different colour pen to the Draw and Write activity from the beginning of the session.

- End the session with *Pass the smile* or a similar closure activity. (For guidance on closure activities see page 44.)

Name: _____   Date: _____

WHAT MAKES A GOOD FRIEND?

Read the sentences and then circle Good or Not good for each one.

1.	Rosie has a friend who talks about their other friends when they are not around and talks about Rosie too when she is not there.	Good	Not good
2.	Leon's friend always pressures him to do things that he doesn't want to do and never takes No for an answer.	Good	Not good
3.	Mary's friend always buys the same clothes as her even though Mary has told her that it makes her very angry.	Good	Not good
4.	John and his best friend always have fun together.	Good	Not good
5.	Mita's friend always makes time for her and listens to her if she is worried about something.	Good	Not good
6.	Tony's friend is always happy for him when good things happen to him.	Good	Not good
7.	Kavita's friend always gets jealous when Kavita gets better marks or when she gets invited to a party on her own.	Good	Not good
8.	Amar's best friend always makes Amar feel good about himself.	Good	Not good
9.	Nicki totally trusts her friend.	Good	Not good
10.	Theo's friend always helps him to do the right thing so that Theo doesn't ever get into trouble.	Good	Not good

How did you do? Here are the right answers:

1. Not good; 2. Not good; 3. Not good; 4. Good; 5. Good; 6. Good; 7. Not good; 8. Good; 9. Good; 10. Good;

If you scored less than five, think very carefully. Is it time you had a talk with your friend? Or talk to an adult you trust.

Copyright © Ruth MacConville 2017

Name: _____ Date: _____

IT'S GOOD NEWS

Think about how your partner communicated with you during your conversation and then answer the following questions giving a Yes or No for each item.

Did my partner:	Yes/No	Comments
use a greeting to open the conversation		
face me		
make eye contact		
speak clearly		
respect my personal space		
listen and show interest while I was speaking		
interrupt		
celebrate my good news		
fidget		
yawn		
look bored		
encourage me to keep talking		
ask me questions		
end the conversation politely		

Circle the words which describe your partner:

friendly   shy   bored   relaxed   nervous   unfriendly
cheerful   confident   fun   embarrassed

How did you rate this conversation overall?

Excellent   Good   Okay   Unsatisfactory

What would you do differently to make future conversations go better?

_____

Copyright © Ruth MacConville 2017

Name: _____ Date: _____

IT'S HOW YOU SAY IT

Read the questions below and circle Yes or No if the question is true about you.

Do you smile when you see a person and catch their eye?	Yes No
Do you look into the eyes of the person that you are talking to?	Yes No
Do you give people compliments that are straight from your heart?	Yes No
Do you smile and say thank you when you get a compliment?	Yes No
Do you make your friends feel good about themselves?	Yes No
Somebody upsets you: do you think carefully about what to do next?	Yes No
Do you let others know that it is sometimes OK to disagree?	Yes No
If you and your friend want different things, do you know how to work things out together?	Yes No
Do you say what you mean?	Yes No

How many times did you circle Yes? _____

If you have got five or more, congratulations, you know how to get your message across.

If you circled No to some questions, use these as ideas to help you to improve your friendship skills.

Copyright © Ruth MacConville 2017

Name: _____ Date: _____

WHAT DID I LEARN?

Name of the session:

1. What did I learn?

2. Something about the lesson that I didn't understand

Copyright © Ruth MacConville 2017

3. One question I have about the lesson is…

4. Next we could…

Copyright © Ruth MacConville 2017

SESSION 15: MY HERO

In this session children are encouraged to identify their heroes or role models (the terms are used interchangeably) and explore their strengths and talents. It will be important to emphasise that heroes and role models come in all different shapes and sizes and from all different walks of life. They can be individuals who are famous or everyday heroes, i.e. people who children know in their daily lives. Having positive role models is central to the theory of self-efficacy (Bandura 1997), i.e. the belief in one's ability to succeed: if they can do it, I can do it as well. Studies suggest that when children notice a person succeeding at something, their confidence in their own abilities increases, and inevitably when they see people failing, their confidence decreases. Positive role models offer children powerful sources of inspiration and hopefulness.

Learning objectives

We are learning to:

- understand why positive role models are important

- identify the positive role models in our lives.

Learning outcomes

I can:

- tell you about the strengths and talents of the individuals who inspire me

- explain what an *everyday hero* is

- understand how recognising the strengths and talents of my heroes inspires me and helps me to feel good about my own strengths and talents.

Resources

Right Now activity:

- My hero

Take Away activity:

- My everyday hero

Key vocabulary

- role model

- hero

- talents

Pre-teaching session

Children with special educational needs and disabilities may benefit from a short pre-teaching session to introduce them to the key vocabulary that is used in this session. (For guidance on differentiation see page 62.)

Introduction (approx. 10 mins)

- Open the session by reviewing the class rules that were agreed in the earlier session. Is there anything that we might like to change, amend or add before we begin the session? Remind the class of the reasons for having rules and how they can support their learning.

- Carry out random pairing so that each child has a Talk Partner for the session. (For guidance on how to make random pairings see page 59.)

- Review the Take Away activity from the previous session.

- Open the session by asking the class for examples of people who they admire.

- Record the children's suggestions in two lists by deciding with the class whether the people they have identified are heroes or everyday heroes, i.e. are they famous people or are they people they know in their daily lives?

Starter activity: Draw and Write activity: My heroes (approx. 10 mins)

Ask the children to draw a picture and add their thoughts on what makes a hero. (For guidance on Draw and Write activities see page 41.)

Class discussion (approx. 10 mins)

Ask the class whether they agree or disagree with the following:

It is important to choose role models:

- who you admire

- who make you feel good about yourself

- who set an example of how you would like to be.

Talk Partner discussion (approx. 5 mins)

With their Talk Partners, ask the class to think about their heroes and discuss:

- whether their hero fits these criteria

- whether their hero has the qualities that they value

- what these qualities are.

Class discussion continued (approx. 10 mins)

Discuss with the class that choosing our role models carefully is important, because the person whom we choose to admire can help us to become the person we want to be.

When we see somebody being successful, their success can help us to think positively: 'If they can do it, I can do it as well.' It is important to choose realistic role models who can help us be the best that we can be. Think about their strengths and ask yourself, are they the strengths that I value and want for myself?

Ask the class to think about whether they would feel happy following in the footsteps of the role models that they have chosen.

Remember that children are likely to benefit from hearing about the role models that you admire.

Right Now activity: My hero

With their Talk Partners, ask the class to take it in turns to talk about a person or character that they like and admire. This can be somebody they know through the media or in their everyday lives who has made good things happen. Then ask them individually to complete the activity sheet *My hero*.

Mid-session learning stop (approx. 5 mins)

Step 1

Randomly choose a child to feed back on this activity. Ask the child to explain:

- where they are up to with completing the task

- if they have any questions or comments

- if they need any advice or help.

Step 2

Ask the rest of the class to reflect on their work in a similar way. Allow the class time to complete the task.

Take Away activity: My everyday hero

Introduce this activity to the class. It involves asking the children to each identify a person in their everyday lives who is a positive role model or what we sometimes call an everyday hero, and getting them to write a paragraph or draw a picture of this person. Why have they chosen these individuals? What are their strengths or special qualities?

List these next to each role model using the following three categories:

- learning strengths

- relationship strengths

- activity strengths.

Take feedback from this activity and add new examples of strengths and positive qualities to the list that was started at the beginning of the session.

Final plenary: reflect and review (approx. 10 mins)

- Revisit the learning objectives for the session with the class and discuss whether the learning outcomes have been met.

- Encourage the class to ask any questions that they have in relation to the session. Children who are able to communicate in writing can be encouraged to submit anonymous questions after the session by using the letter box.

- With their Talk Partners, ask the class to talk through what they have learnt in the session and then individually add new ideas and learning using a different colour pen to the Draw and Write activity from the beginning of the session.

- End the session with *Pass the smile* or a similar closure activity. (For guidance on closure activities see page 44.)

Name: _____ Date: _____

MY HERO

1. Write a paragraph or draw a picture of your hero.

2. My hero's strengths are:

Learning Strengths	Relationship Strengths	Activity Strengths

Copyright © Ruth MacConville 2017

Name: _____ Date: _____

MY EVERYDAY HERO

1. Write a paragraph or draw a picture of your everyday hero.

2. My everyday hero's strengths are:

Learning Strengths	Relationship Strengths	Activity Strengths

Look at www.giraffe.org and www.myhero.com and find some more heroes.

Copyright © Ruth MacConville 2017

SESSION 16: WOOP
Background notes

Making a realistic plan is a fitting activity to mark the end of the programme. In this session the WOOP activity enables children to think about the healthy living skills that they have learnt about in the programme and set a realistic goal for what they would like to achieve in the future. Psychologist and author Jeremy Dean (2013) explains that WOOP is a straightforward, fun way to break a goal into smaller parts, making it easier to achieve. WOOP stands for Wish, Outcome, Obstacle and Plan. There are four steps involved:

1. Children identify their **W**ish, the healthy habit that they would like to achieve.

2. Children then identify the best **O**utcome of that wish, i.e. how their life would be different if they achieved their wish.

3. Children identify the **O**bstacles, the things that may get in the way of them achieving their goal.

4. The final stage is for each child to make a SMART **P**lan.

End of programme celebration

Celebration is a skill. It involves sharing with others and receiving good wishes, praise and congratulations. It is a way of building happy, enjoyable events and therefore happy memories. Happy memories are an important part of a resilient mindset. Positive psychologist Barbara Frederickson (2009) coined the term *peak end rule* to describe the fact that our memories and our evaluation of an event or experience are shaped by its peak times (pleasing or uncomfortable) and by the way it ends (on a high or on a low). Thanking each child by name as their achievements throughout the programme are acknowledged and they are given their individualised certificates, is an effective closure activity for the programme. It is also a rewarding way to express appreciation for each child's active participation in the programme.

Learning objectives

Children will:

- review the healthy living skills that they have learnt about in the programme
- learn how to devise a WOOP plan
- celebrate what they have learnt throughout the programme.

Learning outcomes

I can:

- review what I have learnt about having a positive body image during the programme
- listen to others

- contribute to class discussion

- make a plan to help me reach my healthy living goal

- celebrate my achievements with my class for learning and working well together throughout the programme.

Resources

Right Now activities:

- Ten healthy messages

- WOOP

End of Programme Certificates for each child

Key vocabulary

- review

- plan

- celebrate

Pre-teaching session

Children with special educational needs and disabilities may benefit from a short pre-teaching session to introduce them to the key vocabulary that is used in this session. (For guidance on differentiation see page 62.)

Introduction (approx. 10 mins)

- Open the session by reviewing the class rules that were agreed in the earlier session. Is there anything that we might like to change, amend or add before we begin the session? Remind pupils of the reasons for having rules and how they can support their learning.

- Carry out random pairing so that each child has a Talk Partner for the session (see page 59 for guidance on how to make these pairings).

- Review the Take Away activity from the previous session.

Class discussion (approx. 15 mins)

Explain to the class that this is the last session in the Positive Body Image programme and it is time to think about what we have learnt.

With their Talk Partners, ask the children to list what they have learnt about during the programme. The discussions should include:

- the topics that have been covered

- their views on the success of the activities they have taken part in

- what they have learnt from working together with their Talk Partners and as a whole class.

Right Now activity: What is a positive body image? (approx. 5 mins)

Ask the class to revisit the *Draw and Write* activity *What is a positive body image?* from Session 1 and add to it, with a different colour pen, further learning about the topic since the first session.

Take feedback on this activity.

Right Now activity: Ten healthy messages (approx. 5 mins)

Distribute the *Ten healthy messages* activity sheet to use as a prompt for the goal-setting activity that follows.

Class discussion (approx. 10 mins)

Introduce the WOOP goal-setting activity. It will be important to talk through the four steps of this goal-setting approach with the class. Ensure that the class understands how to make their plan SMART (specific, measurable, achievable, realistic and time bound).

- **W**ish: ask children to identify their wish or goal for the future.

- **O**utcome: if their wish came true or if they achieved their goal, how would their lives be different?

- **O**bstacles: list the things that could stop your wish coming true.

- **P**lan: make a SMART plan.

Right Now activity: WOOP

Each child completes the WOOP activity.

End of programme celebration

The session should end with a small party with music and healthy snacks and drinks to ensure a celebratory ending to the programme.

Certificates

The certificates should be photocopied onto card and signed by the teacher who has delivered the programme, as well as the headteacher. They should be presented to each child individually in recognition of the fact that they have completed the programme. It is important that each child knows that their efforts, contributions and achievements are valued.

End of programme evaluation

Teachers may wish the class to complete this evaluation after the session, which is reproduced on page 46.

Name: _____ Date: _____

TEN HEALTHY MESSAGES

Read the messages and colour the ones that are true for you.

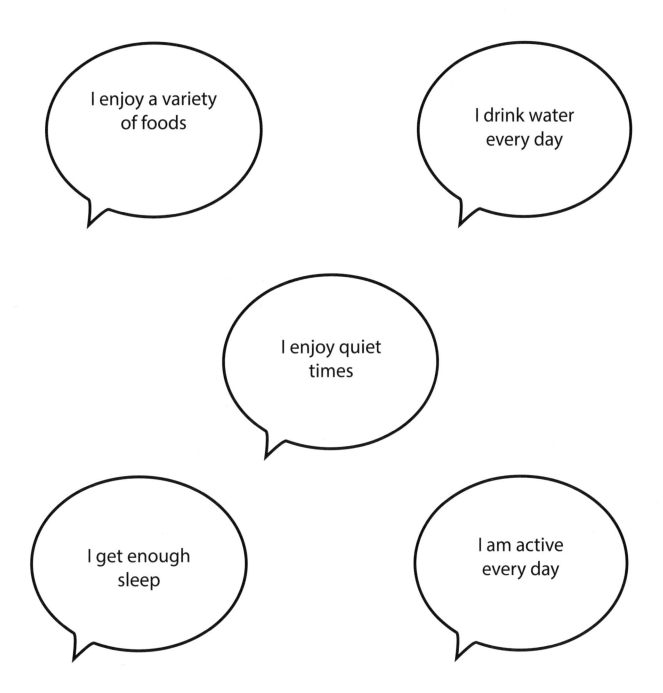

Copyright © Ruth MacConville 2017

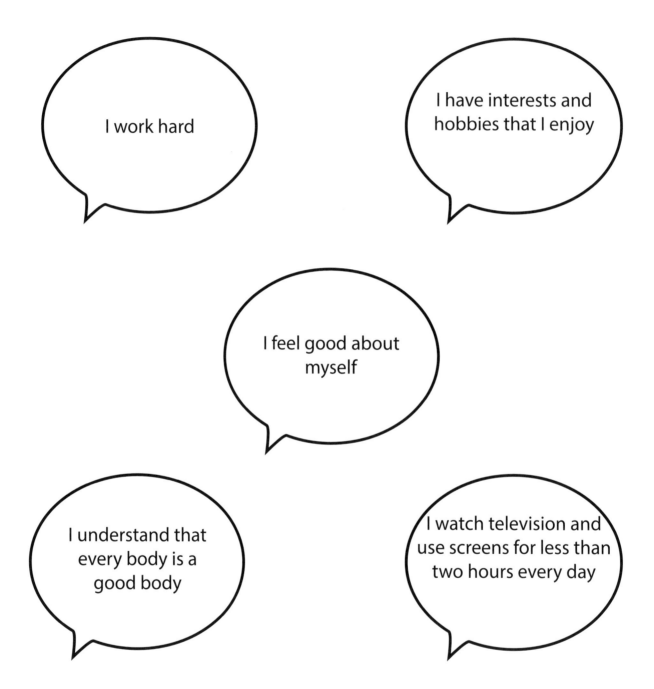

Copyright © Ruth MacConville 2017

Name: _____ Date: _____

WOOP

- **W**ish: Write down your wish for the near future.

- **O**utcome: If your wish came true, how would your life be different?

- **O**bstacles: What could stop your wish coming true? Make a list.

- **P**lan: Make a SMART plan.

A SMART plan

Specific: Write down what it is that you want to achieve. Make sure that your goal is specific.

Measurable: How will you know that you are moving towards achieving your goal? What are the small steps that you want to achieve on the way?

Achievable: Make sure that your goal is not too easy or you will get bored. Make sure that your goal is not too difficult or you may be tempted to give up.

Realistic: Is your goal realistic and something that you really want to happen?

Time bound: Write down the date by which you want to achieve your goal.

Copyright © Ruth MacConville 2017

THIS CERTIFICATE IS AWARDED TO

For successfully completing the
Positive Body Image programme

Congratulations!

Signed   ....
          Teacher

Signed   ....
          Headteacher

School   ....

Date   ....

Copyright © Ruth MacConville 2017

CHAPTER 6

INVOLVING PARENTS AND CARERS

WHY DO WE NEED TO INVOLVE PARENTS?

The engagement of parents in their children's education is recognised to be of utmost importance. Recent and extensive high-quality research confirms that the involvement of parents and carers in their child's learning impacts positively on achievement and social development. The Ofsted Framework (2015) emphasises that engaging with parents to support their children to improve their learning is a key requirement for schools. In order to obtain outstanding judgements in the areas of Effectiveness of Leadership and Management and Quality of Teaching and Learning, schools have to evidence:

- how well leaders engage with parents to support all pupils

- that parents are given guidance about how to support their child to improve

- that leaders use highly successful strategies to engage parents and carers, including those from different groups, in their children's learning in school and at home (in the early years judgement).

Facilitators delivering the Positive Body Image programme need to recognise that parents have a critical role to play in enabling their children to develop the behaviours and attitudes that are promoted by the programme. Although many parents will be reassured to know that specific steps are being taken in school to introduce children to the programme, there will also, inevitably, be parents who, for a variety of reasons, may be concerned about their child's involvement and find the prospect of becoming involved in the programme themselves a worrying or even threatening prospect. It is vital, therefore, that teachers take these concerns into account and are aware of the importance of taking a co-ordinated, systematic, parent-friendly approach to involving *all* parents throughout the planning and the delivery of the programme.

Key tasks will include ensuring that parents are 'onside' and understand the importance of the programme, why it is being run, and the difference that it can make to their own and their children's lives. It will be important for facilitators to convey to parents that an underlying principle on which the programme is based is that of 'first do no harm'. The programme does not address issues relating directly to children's appearance or address issues such as dieting. The emphasis throughout the programme is on building children's self-esteem and resilience and introducing them to the key building blocks of healthy living.

Facilitators will also need to understand how it fits in with the school's overall safeguarding policy and other PSHE programmes.

Although the programme takes a strengths-based approach, facilitators need to be aware that for many parents body image is an emotional and also a sensitive topic and may arouse strong feelings and reactions. They should therefore be familiar with the advice prepared by the PSHE Association (2012): *Handling Sensitive or Controversial Issues*. This guidance is summarised on page 53 of this book. It is also crucial that a supportive, empathic and caring ethos is conveyed to parents throughout all communications.

In order to address concerns from parents that may be triggered by the introduction of the programme, facilitators need to be aware that a key component of the programme, and one that is likely to be welcomed by parents, is the offer of individual meetings for those who have particular concerns that they would like to discuss, on an individual basis, prior to their attendance at the workshop. This offer will be crucial for those who want to talk, in confidence, about their concerns or share their worries about any particular appearance sensitivities that they consider their child may have.

When managing meetings which may involve parents sharing concerns that go beyond queries and questions about the content of the programme, it will be important for teachers to be aware that if there are questions that they cannot answer they should reassure parents that they should seek the advice and guidance of other professionals who are more qualified to help and possibly, with parental permission and depending on professional thresholds, become involved. Facilitators should be familiar with the PSHE guidance on answering children's questions. This guidance is summarised on page 61 of this book and is also relevant to working with adults.

It may also be appropriate in some instances for facilitators to signpost parents to sources of help. A list of organisations and useful websites can be found at the back of this book. Crucially, members of staff who are providing this support need to feel confident in carrying out this role and, as noted above, know that they are strongly supported in real terms to include regular opportunities for debriefing and advice by designated members of the school's senior leadership team.

PRACTICAL CONSIDERATIONS

One of the parent-friendly strategies that has been successful in many primary schools for involving parents in the Positive Body Image programme is to provide a school-based workshop. Involving parents through a practical workshop ensures that they receive a first-hand introduction to the programme, and discussion with the facilitators and other attendees can help to ensure that it is practical and relevant to their child's day-to-day experiences. A workshop will also provide parents with the knowledge and strategies that they can use to support their child throughout the programme and increase their confidence in dealing with challenging situations that may arise. Importantly, a workshop will also provide an opportunity to meet and share experiences with other parents.

Preparation for the workshop must include both practical considerations relating to, for example, room use and resources, as well as reflection on their skills as a facilitator and the need to create a safe, welcoming environment for parents.

It is also important that the facilitator feels able to 'hold' a group and is prepared to deal with any concerns that may arise. This does not mean, of course, that the facilitator will necessarily be able to answer all the questions that are raised by parents, but rather they will know where to go to seek additional help and advice. It is essential therefore that facilitators:

- have the support of the headteacher and the senior leadership team

- do not feel that they have to know the answers to all the questions that parents may raise but know who to refer them to should queries arise, for example relevant members of the senior leadership team or the school's educational or clinical psychologist or counsellor

- are aware of the helpful guidance prepared by the PSHE Association on answering different sorts of questions. Although this guidance was prepared in relation to answering children's questions, it is also relevant to working with parents, especially in relation to how to deal sensitively and confidently with those questions which are difficult to answer. This guidance is summarised on page 61.

It is strongly recommended that two facilitators run the workshop. This could involve a 'lead' facilitator (for example, a teacher or learning mentor) supported by a learning support assistant. Having two facilitators means that there is built-in support for each individual and that one can take on an observer role if appropriate.

The lead facilitator should:

- have experience of delivering meetings and workshops for parents

- have a positive approach and proven skills in relation to promoting social and emotional learning

- understand how emotional literacy promotes mental health and school achievement

- be familiar with the Positive Body Image programme

- be supported by the senior leadership team and have regular opportunities to meet with a designated member of this team for debriefing, to seek advice and to share successes and any concerns that may arise.

PREPARING FOR THE WORKSHOP

When planning a workshop it will be important to:

- send out a letter as early as possible informing parents about the programme and asking for their ideas and thoughts about what topics should be included in the workshop

- inform parents about the workshop that will be held to involve them in the programme (generally holding a workshop during the evening is likely to enable more parents to attend).

In the letter, make it clear that if parents would like to discuss any aspect of the programme in advance of the meeting they are welcome to contact a named person. It will be helpful to provide specific times and ways (phone call, email exchange, meeting) of when this contact could take place. It is hoped that an offer of a meeting with a named member of staff prior to the workshop will reassure and encourage parents, especially those who are concerned about their own or their child's body image issues.

Facilitators need to be aware that initial personal contact is likely to significantly increase parents' confidence and their willingness to be engaged in the programme, as it can provide an opportunity for parents to air any concerns that they may have and ask specific questions that they may be reluctant to raise in a group setting.

Think about the location of the meeting. A large, public hall may not provide a welcoming environment. Depending on the number of attendees, a smaller, more comfortable room in the familiar surroundings of the school will usually be more suitable, as will providing light refreshments such as tea, coffee and biscuits.

Ensure the presence of the headteacher or a member of the senior leadership team to welcome parents and introduce the workshop. Throughout the workshop, allow plenty of time for discussion, comments and questions. Remember to positively reinforce and thank parents for their contributions throughout the meeting.

Be aware that the workshop may raise particular issues for some parents and that they may want to raise issues with you in confidence. If possible, allow time for this directly after the meeting or let parents know that appointment times will be available later in the week or in the fortnight following the workshop.

INTRODUCING THE POSITIVE BODY IMAGE PROGRAMME: A WORKSHOP FOR PARENTS
AIM

The aim of the workshop is to introduce the Positive Body Image programme and explore the ways that parents can support the programme at home.

AGENDA
1. Welcome and introductions

The session should open with a welcome and introductions. The person leading the workshop (ideally, as noted above, this should be the headteacher or member of the senior leadership team) should: introduce him/herself, welcome parents to the workshop, thank them for attending and, time allowing, share with the attendees information such as his/her role in the school and in the delivery of the Positive Body Image programme. The facilitators should then introduce themselves.

Depending on the number of parents attending, parents should then be invited to introduce themselves either to the whole group or to the person sitting next to them, and if they feel comfortable doing so, share any information (such as how many children, occupation, special interests) with the person next to them or with the group.

2. Why are we here?

The purpose of the workshop is to introduce parents to the Positive Body Image programme. Parents are the most important people in a child's life, and their support and involvement in the programme will increase their chances of benefiting from it. Throughout the programme the emphasis is on enabling children to identify their strengths and talents in order to strengthen their sense of identity and healthy self-esteem.

Parents can support the programme by:

- making a habit of noticing and commenting on their child's strengths

- creating opportunities for children to practise the healthy living skills that are introduced throughout the programme

- reinforcing its positive messages.

3. The presentation

The purpose of the presentation is to introduce the Positive Body Image programme and explore with parents how they can support the programme at home. The presentation consists of eight slides, with additional notes and activities to support the facilitator in delivering the presentation.

SLIDE 1

POSITIVE BODY IMAGE FOR KIDS:
A STRENGTHS-BASED CURRICULUM FOR CHILDREN AGED 7–11

Facilitator's notes

The aim of this presentation is to introduce the Positive Body Image programme and explore how you as parents can be involved and support the programme at home. It is important from the beginning of this session to reassure you all that the introduction of the programme is to help our children celebrate their positive body image and build their healthy living skills. The programme is not being introduced in school because of any particular concerns that members of staff may have about individual children.

It is important to emphasise that parents are welcome to ask questions throughout the presentation and that there will be plenty of opportunities for discussion.

The programme is being introduced because as a school we are aware of the increasing advertising pressures on families that emphasise children's appearance over and above their other qualities. This continuous media pressure affects all of us. A report published by the All Party Parliamentary Group on Body Image (APPG 2012) showed that when children are exposed to media celebrating the 'thin ideal' for women's bodies – such as magazines, TV shows and advertising – they experience increased body dissatisfaction, greater negative mood, higher levels of depression and lowered self-esteem. And these negative experiences aren't limited to girls. Thanks to images of slim, muscular men in both media messages and in 'action figure toys', approximately a third of young boys aged between six and eight years indicate their ideal body is thinner than their actual body. The purpose of the Positive Body Image programme is to counteract the negative and damaging effects of exposure to unrealistic media images. It's practically impossible to prevent children from seeing these media images, and to attempt to do so would leave them ill-equipped to enter the adult world and deal with the social world.

It is important to acknowledge that sophisticated marketing techniques have a huge influence on all our children, and the only way to deal with the pressure is to ensure that our children have a strong sense of belonging in their lives, are aware of their strengths and have a healthy self-esteem. Although we are slowly moving towards a place where, thanks to responsible companies, reckless marketing aimed at young children is being stopped, the pressure on children and families can be best negotiated by encouraging our children to see themselves from the inside out rather than from the outside in.

SLIDE 2

What is body image?

Our body image refers to our ideas about how our body looks, how we feel about our appearance and how attractive we feel we are to others.

Anyone, whatever they look like, can have a positive or a negative body image.

Our body image changes in response to others; our family, our friends or the media can all influence our body image.

Facilitator's notes

Body image is a broad concept that refers to the way that individuals think and feel about their appearance. It encompasses ideas about size and shape, skin colour, birthmarks, scars, facial features and clothing. It is also related to personal religious beliefs, physical disabilities and the use of equipment and aids like wheelchairs and hearing aids. Body image is learned.

Studies suggest that concerns about personal appearance seem to emerge around the age of six or seven years, although much younger children are already aware of the 'thin ideal'. There are a range of factors that contribute to how an individual views their appearance, and these factors are intertwined and difficult to separate. One of the most powerful influences is the family environment. Parents are key to children's healthy development, and this includes their body image. Within families, studies suggest that body dissatisfaction is contagious. Friendships are also important, as children watch and listen to their friends. Peer influences can have a strong influence on how children feel about their appearance. They are influenced by 'fat talk' – for example, *'I look so fat.' 'No you don't, I look even fatter'* – and by how much their friends take part in sports and enjoy a healthy lifestyle. Messages from other important adults and the media all play a significant role.

Available at www.jkp.com/voucher using the code MACCONVILLEPOSITIVE

SLIDE 3

Positive body image

Having a positive body image means being happy with how your body actually is.
The effects of a positive body image are far-reaching. Feeling good about one's appearance:

- instils an optimistic attitude

- strengthens social confidence, which in turn attracts friends

- builds self-confidence

- enables an individual to be successful in a variety of domains and have the confidence to participate in a wide range of activities, including sports and other leisure pursuits.

Facilitator's notes

A positive body image enables children to feel good about themselves and supports their mental health and well-being. Children with a positive body image are comfortable with their appearance and think about their body in terms of what it can do, i.e. its functionality, rather than how it looks. This means that their main focus is the way their body enables them to do the things they want to do, like playing sport, dancing and singing, rather than how their body looks. Having a positive body image does not mean, however, that a child is fully satisfied with their appearance but that they concentrate on its assets rather than on its flaws. This positive way of thinking contributes to a positive sense of self-worth. It enables children to be aware of and fulfil their body's needs, and this means that they are more likely to appreciate the value of healthy habits such as exercise and nutritious food choices that enable the body to perform well. Studies suggest, however, that both boys and girls are increasingly experiencing negative thoughts or feelings about their appearance or dissatisfaction with how their bodies look.

A positive body image is inextricably linked to a child's self-esteem. Healthy body esteem is extremely important in becoming an independent, flourishing person. A negative body image contributes to a child's low self-esteem and can trigger depression. Self-esteem is related to self-worth, self-respect, self-awareness, self-image, self-efficacy and self-reliance. Studies suggest that children with positive self-esteem are more likely to do well in school, have a wide range of interests and are less likely to become depressed or develop an eating disorder. They are also more likely to be socially adjusted, to be able to make and keep friends and to establish close emotional bonds as adults. Positive body esteem is therefore extremely important in becoming an independent, healthy person.

Healthy body esteem rests on a strong sense of self – a clear identity and a sense of basic trust and security. These are the qualities which are promoted by the Positive Body Image programme. In addition to promotion of healthy habits, the programme teaches children how to think in a reflective way, to weigh things up and solve problems, and to put effort into the anticipation of a positive outcome. Children who have a positive sense of self are able to use a variety of healthy living skills and strategies, often helped by a reliable parent or other adult who is able to reinforce the child's self-belief and realistic optimism.

Provide an opportunity for parents to ask questions about a positive body image.

SLIDE 4

What is a strengths-based approach?

A strengths-based approach is about helping children to discover and use their individual strengths. Strengths:

- are the interests and abilities which have strong appeal to the child

- bring them success and satisfaction

- create positive energy so that the child is keen to carry on using their strengths in different situations again and again

- enable children to find out more about themselves

- provide positive experiences which create confidence:

  - I did that

  - I made that happen.

Strengths strengthen a child's self-esteem and autonomy and create a sense of achievement.

Facilitator's notes

The Positive Body Image programme focuses on the development of the children's capabilities and competencies to help them solve problems and build healthy habits.

Throughout the programme there is an emphasis on enabling children to identify their strengths and categorise them into learning strengths, relationship strengths and activity strengths (i.e. skills and talents). An emphasis on strengths is important because it is extremely motivating for children (and all of us) to have their stengths identified and acknowledged. It enables children to develop a more positive view of themselves that can be built on and reinforced, thus enabling children to discover and use their personal power positively and productively. Strengths grow with regular use. When we are actively using our strengths, it makes us feel full of energy.

Provide an opportunity for participants to ask questions and discuss with a partner or in a group the sorts of strengths that they have recognised in their children. Take feedback on this discussion.

Available at www.jkp.com/voucher using the code MACCONVILLEPOSITIVE

SLIDE 5
THE POSITIVE BODY IMAGE PROGRAMME

Facilitator's notes

Provide parents with a list of the sessions that form the programme. This can be found on page 75. The facilitator should then briefly describe each session, noting the key learning points from each one.

It will be important to draw parents' attention to Session 5: The real you, which asks children to consider their family traits in terms of their appearance. Parents should be reassured that the sensitivities of the children are taken fully into account with regard to their attendance at this session.

Additionally, it will also be important to reassure parents that throughout the programme children are actively discouraged from disclosing personal information during the sessions and that arrangements are in place should children want to speak in confidence to a member of staff before or after a session. A letter box has also been placed in the classroom should children have questions that they wish to be answered in confidence.

Available at www.jkp.com/voucher using the code MACCONVILLEPOSITIVE

SLIDE 6
THE BOUNCE BACK MUSCLES QUIZ

Facilitator's notes

Distribute a copy of the *Bounce back muscles quiz* to each participant. Explain that this quiz is given to the children in the early stages of the programme in order to draw each child's attention to their strengths and the protective factors that exist in their lives. Most children are bombarded on a daily basis with messages from social networking sites and virtual worlds designed to convince them that the key to their happiness is achieving the *right* appearance and the acquisition of the *right* brands. Studies suggest, however, that relying on one's appearance and believing that buying the right products will make us happy doesn't work. Individuals with materialistic values are actually less happy than those who are not so invested in their appearance and the things that money can buy. The Positive Body Image programme aims to strengthen children's sense of identity and build their self-esteem. It does this by enabling the children to identify their strengths, acknowledge their talents and also recognise the protective factors that exist in their lives such as the people who care for them, both family and friends.

The purpose of the *Bounce back muscles quiz* is to provide children with an opportunity to explore these areas and, throughout the programme, to consciously strengthen them in order to enhance their resilience and make them less vulnerable to the onslaught of commercial marketing.

It will be important to explain to participants that it can be difficult for children – and for all of us – to identify our strengths and our special skills and talents because most of us are not used to thinking about ourselves in this way. We may need a great deal of encouragement in order to be able to do this, and children are usually no different. The key adults in children's lives have a special role in enabling children to identify and name their strengths. If they are unable to do this at first, it is not because they do not have strengths but because they need the encouragement and sometimes the words to name their strengths. An important focus of the programme is to encourage children's ability to recognise and strengthen their skills and talents.

The *Bounce back muscles quiz* consists of four areas:

- I can (my skills, abilities, talents)

- I have (my family, friends)

- I am (my personal qualities, talents and strengths)

- I like (my hobbies, interests and the things that I enjoy doing).

(Adapted from Grotberg 1997)

The quiz that children complete during the session calculates their scores in the four areas. It is not a psychometric test but can give us an indication of the areas where children may need their confidence and self-esteem to be strengthened throughout the programme.

Suggest that participants complete the quiz themselves and then take feedback from them. Complete the activity by reminding participants of the importance of encouraging their children's awareness of their strengths.

SLIDE 7
RECOMMENDED READING AND USEFUL WEBSITES

Facilitator's notes

Distribute a list of recommended reading and useful websites to each participant. Explain that the suggestions of books and websites have been devised to provide parents with further information about the areas that are covered by the Positive Body Image programme in order to help them support their child's learning.

Suggest that participants take a few moments to look at the lists, and provide an opportunity for discussion and questions.

SLIDE 8

Further information and support

Contact:

Email:

Tel:

Facilitator's notes

Reassure parents that if they have any further questions about the programme they should contact a named person in the school.

Remind parents that if they would like to talk to a member of staff about the programme they should telephone or email .... to make an appointment.

Close the workshop by saying that you hope that the workshop has been helpful. Thank participants for attending and for their helpful contributions and participation.

EXAMPLE LETTER TO PARENTS

Dear ....

I am writing to let you know that this term (year) in school we will be introducing the Positive Body Image programme. This programme has been designed to introduce children to the basic building blocks of healthy living. It also focuses on enabling the children to recognise and celebrate their strengths and talents. If you have any ideas or suggestions about topics that you think should be included in the programme, please let your child's teacher know as soon as possible. We welcome your suggestions.

We will be encouraging your child to talk about what they have learnt in the sessions with you at home. The activities that children will be asked to complete in school and at home are an important part of the programme. We will also be asking your child to share these activities with you. It would be very helpful if you could take some time to talk to your child about what they have learnt. You may wish to try out some of the activities yourself.

A workshop has been arranged for parents to learn more about the programme and have the opportunity to ask any questions about the sessions.

The workshop will take place on .... at ....

It will be held in room .... It is intended that the meeting will last for approximately two hours.

I look forward to seeing you at the workshop.

If you would like to meet with a member of staff to talk about the programme before the workshop, please let your child's teacher know or telephone/email the school office. You are welcome to bring your child to this meeting if you think that this would be helpful.

Yours sincerely

....

Copyright © Ruth MacConville 2017

FURTHER INFORMATION

FOR CHILDREN
General advice

www.Childline.org.uk

You can talk to ChildLine about anything – whether you're feeling stressed, anxious, lonely or down. Whatever it is, they can help. ChildLine is a private and confidential service. This means that whatever you say stays between you and ChildLine. Call ChildLine free on 0800 1111. Calls are confidential and won't appear on the phone bill, including mobiles.

www.bbc.co.uk/radio1/advice

Helping you get through life: categories include relationships, bullying, your body, your health and well-being.

Advice on staying healthy

www.girlshealth.gov (US site)

Be healthy, be happy, be you. A site designed to promote healthy, positive behaviours in girls. It provides reliable, useful information on the health issues they will face as they grow up and tips on handling relationships with family and friends at school and at home.

Staying safe online

www.kidsmart.org.uk

Kidsmart is an award-winning practical internet safety programme website for children, parents and schools produced by the children's internet charity Childnet International.

www.childnet.com/young-people

The aim of this site is to make the internet a great and safe place for children and young people. Find the latest information on the sites and services that you like to use, plus information about mobiles, gaming downloads, social networking and lots more.

www.thinkuknow.co.uk

Find the latest information on the sites that you like to visit. Find out what's good, what's not and what you can do about it. Most importantly, there's also a place which anyone can use to report if they feel uncomfortable or worried about someone they are chatting to online.

Bullying

www.kidscape.org.uk

Kidscape equips children and young people with the skills to tackle bullying and safeguarding across the UK.

www.youngminds.org.uk

Young Minds is the voice for children and young people's mental health and well-being. It offers information to parents and professionals about young people's and children's mental and emotional well-being.

Recommended reading

You are a Social Detective: Explaining Social Thinking to Kids. Michelle Garcia Winner and Pamela Crooke, The North River Press: www.northriverpress.com, www.socialthinking.com

Cherish Today: A Celebration of Life's Moments. Kristina Evans and Bryan Collier.

How 2B Happy : -) Get the Happy Habit. J. Alexander, A & C Black.

Jump at the Sun. Hyperion Books for Children, New York.

All Kinds of Ways to be Smart! Judi Lalli, Kagan Publishing: www.KaganOnline.com

I Like Being Me: Poems for Children about Feeling Special, Appreciating Others and Getting Along. Judi Lalli, free spirit publishing: www.freespirit.com

Dr Christian's Guide to Dealing with the Tricky Stuff. Dr Christian Jessen, Scholastic: www.scholastic.co.uk

FOR PARENTS
Body image

www.aboutface.org

About-Face is a site that aims to equip women and girls with the tools to understand and resist harmful media messages that affect their self-esteem and body image.

www.proud2bme.org

An online community created by teens that covers everything from fashion and beauty to news, culture and entertainment – all with the goal of promoting positive body image and encouraging healthy attitudes about food and weight.

www.bodygossip.org

A campaign which explores people's experiences of body confidence.

www.changingfaces.org.uk/Home

A charity for people and families who are living with conditions, marks or scars that affect their appearance.

www.dove.us/Our-mission/Girls-Self-Esteem/Ger-Involved/default.aspx

Practical resources for parents and teachers to boost self-esteem.

Mental health and well-being

www.youngminds.org.uk

The voice for young people's mental health and well-being. The UK's leading charity committed to improving the emotional well-being and mental health of children and young people. Provides expert knowledge to parents and professionals. Parents' helpline: 0808 8025544, Monday–Friday, 9.30am–4pm.

www.mind.org.uk

Provides advice and support to empower anyone experiencing a mental health problem. Mind's website features helpful ideas on increasing self-esteem.

Parenting

www.empoweredparents.com

www.familylives.org.uk

A national family support charity providing help and advice on all aspects of family life. It believes that happy children come from happy families. It provides a 24 hours a day, 7 days a week helpline: 0808 8002222.

www.mumsnet.com

Mumsnet aims to make parents' lives easier and believes that pooling knowledge and wisdom helps to do this.

Staying safe online

www.commonsensemedia.org

An organization dedicated to improving the lives of kids, families and educators by providing the trustworthy information and the independent voice that they need to thrive in the digital world.

www.mediawatchuk.org

Campaigns for socially responsible media and against content which is potentially harmful.

www.kidsmart.org.uk

An internet safety programme website for parents, children and schools produced by the children's charity Childnet International.

Health

www.kidsandnutrition.co.uk

Advice for parents about encouraging a positive body image in your child.

www.cyh.com

The Child and Youth Health website where you will find a wealth of news and practical health information for parents, carers and young people.

www.healthykids.nsw.gov.au (Australian site)

A 'one-stop shop' of information for parents, carers, children and teens and also teachers and childcare workers about healthy eating and physical activity.

www.gosh.nhs.uk

General health advice produced by the staff at Great Ormond Street Hospital (GOSH). It's packed with top tips to help children and young people live a healthy life as they grow up.

Find information on how to improve your diet, the benefits of doing regular exercise and advice on looking after your mental health.

Get moving

www.nhs.uk/change4life/Pages/be-more-active.aspx

Easy ways to help children to get more active.

www.nhs.uk/livewell/fitness/pages/physical-activity-guidelines-for-young-people.aspx

Fun dancing games.

www.bhf.org.uk/get-involved/events/school-events/jump-rope-forheart

Skipping games.

www.nhs.uk/change4life/Pages/walk4life-supporter-resources.aspx

Walking.

www.nhs.uk/change4life/Pages/be-more-active.aspx

Family activities.

Healthy eating

www.foodafactoflife.org.uk

Food a Fact of Life: free information and resources about healthy eating, cooking, food and farming for children aged 3–18 years.

www.eatseasonably.co.uk

Eat Seasonably Calendar: What to eat now? What to grow now?

www.nhs.uk/Livewell/Goodfood/Pages/the-eatwell-guide.aspx

The Eat Well Guide: Eat a Balance of Foods.

Recommended reading
Books

Real Kids Come in All Sizes: 10 Essential Lessons to Build Your Child's Body Esteem. Kathy Kater, A Lark Production, Broadway Books: www.broadwaybooks.com

Practical Wisdom for Parents: Raising Self-Confident Children in the Preschool Years. Nancy Schulman and Ellen Birnbaum, Vintage Books: www.vintagebooks.com, www.practicalwisdomforparents.com

The Me, Me, Me Epidemic: A Step by Step Guide to Raising Capable Grateful Kids in an Over-Entitled World. Amy McCready, Jeremy P. Tarcher/Penguin.

Starting Kids Off Right: How to Raise Confident Children who can Make Friends and Build Healthy Relationships. Stephen Nowicki Jr, Marshall P. Duke, Amy Van Buren, Peachtree: www.peachtree-online.com

Talking to Tweens: Getting it Right Before it Gets Rocky with Your 8- to 12-Year-Old. Elizabeth Hartley-Brewer, Da Capo Press: www.dacapopress.com

First Bite: How We Learn to Eat. Bee Wilson, Fourth Estate: www.4thestate.co.uk

Girls Uninterrupted: Steps for Building Stronger Girls in a Challenging World. Tanith Carey, Icon Books: www.iconbooks.com

Girls without Limits: Helping Girls Achieve Healthy Relationships, Academic Success, and Interpersonal Relationships. Lisa Hinkelman, Corwin: www.corwin.com

The Big Disconnect: Protecting Childhood and Family Relationships in the Digital Age. Catherine Steiner-Adair, Harper: www.harpercollins.com, www.catherinesteineradair.com

Calmer Easier Happier Screen Time. For Parents of Toddlers to Teens: A Guide to Getting Back in Charge of Technology. Noel Janis-Norton, Yellow Kite: www.hodder.co.uk

FOR TEACHERS AND OTHER PROFESSIONALS
Positive Psychology
Books

Positive Psychology in a Nutshell: A Balanced Introduction to the Science of Optimal Functioning. Ilona Boniwell, Personal Well-Being Centre.

Flourish: A New Understanding of Happiness and Well-Being – and How to Achieve Them. Martin E.P. Seligman, Nicholas Brealey Publishing.

The Optimistic Child: A Proven Program to Safeguard Children Against Depression and Build Lifelong Resilience. Martin E.P. Seligman, Harper Perennial.

What Children Need to be Happy, Confident and Successful: Step by Step Positive Psychology to Help Children Flourish. Jeni Hooper, Jessica Kingsley Publishers.

Celebrating Strengths: Building Strengths-Based Schools. Jennifer M. Fox-Eades, CAPP Press.

Websites

www.positivepsychology.org.uk

www.authentichappiness.org

www.centreforconfidence.co.uk

www.coachingtowardshappiness.com

www.livingvalues.net

Cognitive Behaviour Therapy

Think Good-Feel Good: A Cognitive Behaviour Therapy Workbook for Children and Young People. Paul Stallard, John Wiley & Sons.

No More Stinking Thinking: A Workbook for Teaching Children Positive Thinking. J. Altiero, Jessica Kingsley Publishers.

Resilience

Books

How Children Succeed: Grit, Curiosity and the Hidden Power of Character. Paul Tough, Houghton Mifflin Harcourt.

A Short Introduction to Promoting Resilience in Children. Colby Pearce, Jessica Kingsley Publishers.

Building Resilience: A Skills Based Programme to Support Achievement in Young People. Ruth MacConville, Speech Mark Publishing.

Websites

www.bounceback.com.au

www.howtothrive.org

newsletters@drrobertbrooks.com

www.boingboing.org.uk/index.php/resources

www.youthbeyondblue.com/do-something-about-it/treatments-for-anxiety-and-depression

Mindfulness

Books

The Art of Mindfulness for Children: Mindfulness Exercises that will Raise Happier, Confident, Compassionate, and Calmer Children. Alisa Reddy. Available on Amazon UK.

Mindfulness: Finding the Magic in Everyday Moments. Alisa Reddy. Available on Amazon UK.

Evidence on the Wellbeing and Performance of School Staff. Katherine Weare, Mindfulness in Schools Project in Association with the University of Exeter.

Websites

www.mindful.org/two-minutes-for-mindfulness

www.mindfulnessinschools.org/what-is-b

www.mindfulnessteachersuk.org.uk

www.getsomeheadspace.com

www.headspace.com/kids/subscribe

Developing Growth Mindsets

Books

I Can't Do This and The Mindset Melting Pot: A Collection of Teacher Inspired Ideas to Create a Growth Mindset. K.J. Walton. Both books are available to buy at www.growthmindset.org; see also that website for how to use them.

Mindset: The New Psychology of Success. Carol Dweck, Ballantine Books.

Websites

www.mindsetworks.com

Practical resources to enable schools to build a growth mindset.

www.practicalsavvy.com

Excellent growth mindset posters can be purchased here.

www.zazzle.com

Purchase growth mindset posters here as well.

www.tpet.co.uk

Teacher's Pet Website for inspirational PSHE posters and activities.

Ted Talk

www.ted.com

Carol Dweck: The Power of Believing that You Can Improve, December 2014.

Assessment

Active Learning through Formative Assessment and Outstanding Formative Assessment: Culture and Practice. Shirley Clarke, Hodder Education. Both of these books and a DVD are available from www.shirleyclarke-education.org.

Supporting Different Learning Needs

Special Needs: What to Know and What to Do. The Professional Development File for All Staff. Ruth MacConville.

www.optimus-education.com/shop

Teach to Inspire.

Common SENse for the Inclusive Classroom – How Teachers Can Maximise Existing Skills to Support Special Educational Needs. Richard Hanks, Jessica Kingsley Publishers.

REFERENCES

Academies Act (2010) Available at www.legislation.gov.uk/ukpga/2010/32, accessed on 24 May 2016.

Acuff, D.S. and Reiher, R.H. (2005) *Kidnapped: How Irresponsible Marketers are Stealing the Minds of Your Children.* Chicago: Dearborn Trade Publishing.

Alderfer, L. and MacLean, K.L. (2011) *Mindful Monkey, Happy Panda.* Sommerville, MA: Wisdom Publications.

Allan, J. (1999) *Actively Seeking Inclusion: Pupils with Special Needs in Mainstream Schools.* London: Falmer Press.

American Psychological Association (2007) *Task Force on the Sexualization of Girls: Report of the APA Task Force on the Sexualization of Girls.* Washington DC: APA.

All Party Parliamentary Group on Body Image (APPG) (2012) *Reflections on Body Image.* London: YMCA.

Asher, S.R., Parker, J.G., Walker, D.L. (1996) 'Distinguishing Friendship from Acceptance: Implications for Interventions and Assessment.' In W.M. Bukowski, A.F. Newcomb, W.W. Hartup (eds) *The Company They Keep: Friendship During Childhood and Adolescence.* New York: Cambridge University Press.

Ausubel, D.P., Novak, J., Hanesian, H. (1978) 'Educational Psychology: A Cognitive View' in Clarke, S. (2014) *Outstanding Formative Assessment: Culture and Practice.* London: Hodder Education.

Bamford, B. (2015) 'Mental health and young people – the next steps in tackling body image dissatisfaction.' *Mental Health and Young People: Promoting a Positive and Healthy Body Image.* A Public Policy Exchange Symposium, 8 October.

Bandura, A. (1997) *Self-Efficacy: The Exercise of Control.* New York: Worth Publishers.

Benelam, B. (2009) 'Satiation, satiety, and their effects on eating behaviour.' *British Nutrition Foundation Bulletin, 4,* 126–173.

Boniwell, I. and Ryan, L. (2012) *Personal Well-Being Lessons for Secondary Schools: Positive Psychology in Action for 11–14 Year Olds.* Berkshire: McGraw Hill Open University Press.

British Council (n.d.) *Guidance on Handling Disclosures from a child.* Available at: www.britishcouncil.org/education/accreditation/information-centres/care-children-careofunder18s-GuidanceonHandlingdisclosuresfromachild, accessed on 14 September 2016.

Brooks, L. (2006) *The Story of Childhood: Growing Up in Modern Britain.* London: Bloomsbury Publishing.

Brooks, R. (2015) Monthly article: *Positive Emotions and Purpose in the Classroom,* available from newsletters@drrobertbrooks.com.

Brooks, R. and Goldstein, S. (2001) *Raising Resilient Children: Fostering Strength, Hope and Optimism in Our Children.* New York: Wiley.

Brooks, R. and Goldstein, S. (2003) *Nurturing Resilience in Our Children: Answers to the Most Important Parenting Questions.* New York: McGraw-Hill.

Brooks, R. and Goldstein, S. (2013) *Handbook of Resilience in Children,* 2nd edition. New York: Springer.

Brown, B. (2015) *Rising Strong.* London: Vermilion.

Cash, T.F. (2008) *The Body Image Workbook: An Eight-Step Program for Learning to Like Your Looks,* second edition. California: New Harbinger Publications.

Children's Act (2004) Available at www.education.gov.uk/publications/eOrderingDownload/DFES-0036-2007.pdf, accessed on 24 May 2016.

Clarke, S. (2014) *Outstanding Formative Assessment: Culture and Practice.* London: Hodder Education.

Collins-Donnelly, K., (2014) *Banish Your Body Image Thief: A cognitive behaviour therapy workbook on building positive body image for young people.* London: Jessica Kingsley Publishers.

Dalton, S. (2004) *Our Overweight Children: What Parents, Schools and Communities Can Do to Control the Fatness Epidemic.* Berkeley: University of California Press

Dean, J. (2013) *Making Habits, Breaking Habits: How to Make Changes that Stick.* London: OneWorld Publications.

Department of Health (2004) *At Least Five a Week: Evidence of the Impact of Physical Activity and its Relationship to Health.* A report by the Chief Medical Officer.

Department for Education (2015) *Keeping Children Safe in Education. Statutory Guidance for Schools and Colleges on Safeguarding and Safer Recruitment.* Ref: DFE-00129-2015.

Department for Education (2015) *Working Together to Safeguard Children. Statutory Guidance on Interagency Working to Safeguard and Promote the Welfare of Children.* Ref: DFE-00130-2015.

Department for Education and Employment (2000) *Sex and Relationship Education Guidance.* London: DfEE.

Dohnt, H.K. and Tiggemann, M. (2005) 'Peer influences, body dissatisfaction and dieting awareness in young girls.' *British Journal of Developmental Psychology, 23,* 1, 103–116.

Dweck, C.S. (2000) *Self-Theories: Their Role in Motivation, Personality and Development.* Hove: Psychology Press.

Dweck, C.S. (2006) *Mindset.* New York: Random House.

Education Act (2002) Available at www.legislation.gov.uk/ukpga/2002/32/section/78, accessed on 24 May 2016.

Elias, M.J., Tobias, S.E., Friedlander, B.S. (1999) *Emotionally Intelligent Parenting: How to Raise a Self-Disciplined, Responsible, Socially Skilled Child.* New York: Three Rivers Press.

Fox, J. (2009) *How to Develop Your Child's Strengths: A Guide for Parents and Teachers.* New York: Viking Penguin.

Fox-Eades, J. (2008) *Celebrating Strengths: Building Strengths-Based Schools.* Coventry: CAPP Press.

Frederikson, B. (2009) *Positivity: Groundbreaking Research to Release Your Inner Optimist.* New York: Crown Publishers.

Gable, S., Reiss, H.T., Impett, E., Asher, E.R. (2004) 'What do you do when things go right? The intrapersonal and interpersonal benefits of sharing positive events.' *Journal of Personality and Social Psychology, 87,* 228–245.

Girlguiding UK (2014) 'What girls think – the 2014 Girls' Attitudes Survey.' Available at www.girlguiding.org.uk/pdf/7037c_GC_WhatGirlsThink.pdf, accessed on 1 April 2016.

Greenberg, M., Domilrovich, C., Bunbarger, B. (2001) 'The prevention of mental disorders in school-aged children: current state of the field.' *Prevention and Treatment, 4* (Article 1).

Greenberg, M., Weissberg, R., O'Brien, M., Zins, J. *et al.* (2003) 'Enhancing school-based prevention and youth development through coordinated social, emotional and academic learning.' *American Psychologist, 58,* 466–474.

Grogan, S. (1999) *Body Image: Understanding Body Dissatisfaction in Men, Women and Children.* London: Routledge.

Grogan, S. (2006) 'Body image and health: contemporary perspectives.' *Journal of Health Psychology, 11,* 4, 523–530.

Grotberg, E. (1997) 'The International Resilience Project.' In B. Daniel and S. Wassell (2002) *The School Years: Assessing and Promoting Resilience in Vulnerable Children 2.* London: Jessica Kingsley Publishers.

Hargreaves, E.H. and Tiggemann, M. (2003) 'The effect of "thin ideal" television commercials on body dissatisfaction and schema activation during early adolescence.' *Journal of Youth and Adolescence, 32,* 5, 367–373.

Harter, S. (1999) *The Construction of Self: A Developmental Perspective.* New York: The Guilford Press.

Hartley-Brewer, E. (2005) *Talking to Tweens: Getting it Right Before it gets Rocky with Your 8- to 12-Year-Old.* Cambridge, MA: Da Capo Press Books.

Hattie, J. (2012) *Visible Learning for Teachers: A Synthesis of Over 800 Meta-Analyses Relating to Achievement.* London: Routledge.

Herbert, P.C. and Lohrmann, D.K. (2011) 'It's all in the delivery! An analysis of instructional strategies from effective health education curricula.' *Journal of School Health, 81,* 258–264.

Hughes, G. (2011) 'Aiming for personal best: a case for introducing ipsative assessment in higher education.' *Studies in Higher Education, 36,* 3, 353–367.

Hutchinson, N. and Calland, C. (2011) *Body Image in the Primary School.* Abingdon: David Fulton Books, Routledge.

Jensen, B.B. and Kostarova-Unkovska, L. (1998) Evaluation in collaboration with students. Workshop on practice of evaluation at a health-promoting school: Models, experiences and perspectives. Quoted in S. Roffey (2011) *Changing Behaviour in Schools: Promoting Positive Relationships and Wellbeing.* London: Sage Publications.

Johnson, S.L. (2000) 'Improving preschoolers' self-regulation of energy intake.' *Pediatrics, 106,* 1429–1435.

Kater, K. (2004) *Real Kids Come in All Sizes: 10 Essential Lessons to Build Your Child's Body Esteem.* New York: Broadway Books.

Kazdin, A.E. and Weisz, J.R. (1998) 'Identifying and developing empirically supported child and adolescent treatments.' *Journal of Consulting and Clinical Psychology, 66,* 19–36.

Knobloch-Westerwick, S. and Crane, J. (2012) 'A losing battle: effects of prolonged exposure to thin ideal images on dieting and body satisfaction.' *Communication Research, 39,* 1, 79–102.

Lieberman, M.D. (2013) *Social: Why Our Brains are Wired to Connect*. New York: Broadway Books.

MacConville, R.M. (2007) *Looking at Inclusion: Listening to the Voices of Young People*. London: Paul Chapman Publishing.

MacConville, R.M. (2008) *How to Make Friends: Building Resilience and Supportive Peer Groups*. London: Sage Publications.

MacLean, K.L. (2004) *Peaceful Piggy Meditation*. Illinois: Albert Whitman & Company.

Masten, A.S. (2001) 'Ordinary magic: resilience processes in development.' *American Psychologist, 56*, 227–238.

Masten, A.S. (2014) *Ordinary Magic: Resilience in Development*. New York: The Guilford Press.

Mayo, E. and Nairn, A. (2009) *Consumer Kids: How Big Business is Grooming Our Children for Profit*. London: Constable & Robinson.

McCabe, M.P., Ricciardelli, L.A., Holt, K. (2005) 'A longitudinal study to explain strategies to change weight and muscles among normal weight and overweight children.' *Appetite, 45*, 3, 225–234.

Mindfulness in Schools Project (undated) Available at www.mindfulnessinschools.org, accessed on 24 May 2016.

Mischel, W. (2014) *The Marshmallow Test: Understanding Self-Control and How to Master It*. London: Bantam Press.

Morris, I. (2009) *Teaching Happiness and Wellbeing in Schools*. London: Continuum Books.

National Institute for Health and Care Excellence (2005) *Obsessive Compulsive Disorder and Body Dysmorphic Disorder treatment*. NICE Guidelines (CG3).

Neumark-Sztainer, D. (2005) *I'm, Like, So Fat! Helping Your Teen Make Healthy Choices about Eating and Exercise in a Weight Obsessed World*. New York: The Guilford Press.

Ofsted (2004) *Promoting and Evaluating Pupils' Spiritual, Moral, Social and Cultural Development*. Ofsted.

Ofsted (2015) *School Inspection Framework*. Gov.uk.

Orbach, S. (2010) *Bodies*. London: Profile Books.

Peterson, C. and Seligman, M. (2004) *Character Strengths and Virtues: A Classification and Handbook*. Washington DC: American Psychological Association.

Phillips, K.A. (2005) *The Broken Mirror: Understanding and Treating Body Dysmorphic Disorder*. Oxford: Oxford University Press.

PSHE Association (undated) *Teacher Guidance: Key Standards in Teaching About Body Image*. Available at www.pshe-association.org.uk, accessed on 24 May 2016.

PSHE Association (2007) *Assessment in PSHE: Putting it into Practice, A CPD Handbook*. PSHE Association.

PSHE Association (2012) *Handling Sensitive or Controversial Issues*. Available at www.pshe-association.org.uk, accessed on 24 May 2016.

PSHE Association (2013) *Answering Children's Questions*. Available at www.pshe-association.org.uk, accessed on 24 May 2016.

PSHE Association (2014) *PSHE Association Programme of Study for PSHE Education (Key Stages 1–4)*. Available at www.pshe-association.org.uk/curriculum-and-resources/resources/pshe-education-programme-study-key-stages-1%E2%80%934, accessed on 24 May 2016.

PSHE Association (2015) *Teacher Guidance in Teaching About Body Image*. Available at www.pshe-association.org.uk, accessed on 24 May 2016.

PSHE Association (2016) *PSHE Education Character Curriculum Planning Toolkit, Section 3 PSHE Education Character Curriculum: Theoretical Context and Evidence Base*. PSHE Association.

PSHE Association (2016) *PSHE Education Character Curriculum Planning Toolkit, Section 4 PSHE Education Character Curriculum: Practical Guidance for Delivery*. Available at www.pshe-association.org.uk, accessed on 24 May 2016.

Public Health England (2014) *The Link between Pupil Health and Wellbeing and Attainment: A Briefing for Head Teachers, Governors and Staff in Education Settings*. Available at www.gov.uk/phe, PHE Publications Gateway Number 2014491.

QCA (2004) *Whole School Development in Assessment for Learning: Unit 5*. Crown Copyright.

QCA (2005) *PSHE at Key Stages 1–4: Guidance on Assessment, Recording and Reporting*. QCA website.

Radford, A. (2015) 'Beating eating disorders.' *Mental Health and Young People: Promoting a Positive and Healthy Body Image*. A Public Policy Exchange Symposium, 8 October.

Roffey, S. (2011) *Changing Behaviour in Schools: Promoting Positive Relationships and Wellbeing*. London: Sage Publications.

Roth, A. and Fonagy, P. (1996) *What Works for Whom? A Critical Review of Psychotherapy Research*. New York: Guilford Press.

Ryan, R.M. and Deci, E.L. (2000) 'Self-determination theory and the facilitation of intrinsic motivation, social development and well-being.' *American Psychologist, 55*, 68–78.

Schildrer, P., (1937) *The Image and Appearance of the Human Body: Studies in the constructive energies of the psyche*. London: K. Paul, Trench, Trübner and Company Ltd.

Schor, J.B. (2004) *Born to Buy*. New York: Scribner.

Segal, J. (1988) 'Teachers have enormous power in affecting a child's self-esteem.' *Brown University Child Behavior and Development 10*, 1–3.

Seligman, M.E.P. (1995) *The Optimistic Child*. New York: Houghton Mifflin.

Seligman, M.E.P. (2008) *The New Era of Positive Psychology*. Available at www.ted.com/talks/martin_seligman_on_the_state_of_psychology, accessed on 1 April 2016.

Seligman, M.E.P. (2011) *Flourish: A New Understanding of Happiness and Wellbeing and How to Achieve Them*. London: Nicholas Brearley Publishing.

Semple, R.J. and Lee, J. (2011) *Mindfulness-Based Cognitive Therapy for Anxious Children: A Manual for Treating Childhood Anxiety*. Oaklands, CA: Harbinger.

Straube, T., Sauer, A., Miltner, W.H.R. (2011) 'Brain activation during direct and indirect processing of positive and negative words.' *Behavioural Brain Research, 222*, 1, 66–72.

Syvertsen, A.K., Roehlkepartain, E.C., Scales, P.C. (2012) *The American Family Assets Study*. Available at www.search-institute.org, accessed on 1 April 2016.

Tantleff-Dunn, S. and Hayes, S. (2010) 'Am I too fat to be a princess? Examining the effects of popular children's media on young girls' body image.' *British Journal of Developmental Psychology, 28*, 2, 413–426.

Thuen, E., & Bru E., 2009, Are changes in students' perceptions of the learning environment related to changes in emotional and behavioural problems? *School Psychology International, 30*, 2, 115- 36

Tough, P. (2012) *How Children Succeed: Grit, Curiosity and the Hidden Power of Character*. New York: Houghton Mifflin Harcourt.

Turner, S. (2014) 'Mindfulness.' *Juno, 37*, 19–21.

Tylka, T.L. (2011) 'Positive Psychology Perspectives on Body Image.' In T.F. Cash and L. Smolak (eds) *Body Image: A Handbook of Science, Practice and Prevention*. New York: The Guilford Press.

Wallace, S.A., Crown, J.M., Cox, A.D., Berger, M. (1995) *Epidemiologically Based Needs Assessment: Child and Adolescent Mental Health*. Wessex Institute of Public Health.

Weichselbaum, E. and Buttriss, J.L. (2014) 'Diet, nutrition and school children: an update.' *Nutrition Bulletin, 39*, 1, 9–73.

Wells, J., Barlow, J., Stewart-Brown, S. (2003) 'A systematic review of the universal approaches to mental health promotion in schools.' *Health Education, 1303*, 4, 97–220.

Wertheim, E. and Paxton, S. (2009) 'Body Image in Girls.' In L. Smolak and J.K. Thompson (eds) *Body Image, Eating Disorders and Obesity in Youth: Assessment, Prevention and Treatment, second edition*. Washington DC: American Psychological Association.

Wilson, T. (2011) *Redirect: The Surprising New Science of Psychological Change*. London: Allen Lane.

INDEX

A Really Fun Time activity 157
active learning strategies 35
    staff training on 77
Acuff, Daniel 168
Alderfer, Lauren 114
All About Me activity 126
All Party Parliamentary Group on Body Image
    (APPG) 20, 65, 71, 72, 73, 230
Allan, J. 19
American Psychological Association 18
Are You a Good Sport? activity 158
Asher, S.R. 202
assessment
    of Positive Body Image programme 44–7
At Least Five a Week (Department of Health) 143
At My Very Best activity 112
Ausubel, D.P. 40

Bamford, Byrony 11
Bandura, A. 211
Barlow, J. 39
Benelam, B. 161
body dismorphic disorder (BDD) 15–16, 67
body dissatisfaction
    All Party Parliamentary Group on Body Image 20
    causes of 16–19
    body dismorphic disorder 15–16, 67
    description of 14–15
    and images of disability 19
    resilience building 21–2
body image
    concept of 11
    parental training on 231
    positive body image 12–13, 68
    and self-esteem 11–12, 68
    staff training on 67–75
Box Breathing activity 119
British Council 53

Brooks, Libby 16
Brooks, Robert 21, 37, 56, 89, 143
Brown, B. 112
Bru, E. 55
Build Your Bounce Back Muscles
    links to curriculum 25
    Look the Part: The High-Power Pose activity 102
    My Bounce Back Muscles activity 95–7
    My Bounce Back Muscles Quiz 98
    My Bounce Back Muscles Record Sheet 100
    My Bounce Back Shield activity 99
    Storyboard – Bounce Back: Bounce
        Forward activity 101
    structure of 89–94
Bunbarger, B. 39
Buttriss, J.L. 38

Calland, C. 18, 19
CASEL 56
Cash, Thomas 11, 16, 17
Catch That Thought activity 192
Celebrate All the Things Your Body
    Can Do activity 129
celebrations
    staff training on 79
    and WOOP 217, 219
certificates 219–20, 224
*Changing Behaviour in Schools: Promoting Positive
    Relationships and Wellbeing* (Roffey) 59
Children's Manifesto activity 175
Clarke, S. 42, 56, 58, 60
co-operative marking 46
cognitive behaviour therapy (CBT) 37–8, 187, 196
Collins-Donnelly, Kate 12, 14
Common Sense Media 19
confidentiality 50–3
Crane, J. 18
curriculum
    links to of Positive Body Image programme 23–34

Dalton, Sharron 17
Dean, Jeremy 217
Deci, E.L. 55
Department of Education 8
Department for Education and Employment 51
Department of Health 143
different learning needs
    in Positive Body Image programme 62–3
disability
    and body dissatisfaction 19
    in Positive Body Image programme 63
disclosures 51–3
distancing techniques 51
Dohnt, H.K. 14
Domilrovich, C. 39
Draw and Write activities
    in Have Fun 153
    in Healthy Eating Habits: Three to Remember 131
    in How to be a Friend 204
    in Introduction to Positive Body
        Image Programme 82
    in My Hero 212
    in Pictures, Pictures Everywhere! 181–2
    in Positive Body Image programme 41
    in The Real You 123
    in Think Twice 170
    whole school approach 38
Dweck, Carol 21–2, 57, 58

Eat a Mix of Foods Every Day activity 137
Elias, M.J. 116
evaluation
    of Positive Body Image programme 44–7
    and WOOP 220

facilitator reflection 48–50
Five Categories of Movement activity 148–9
fixed mindsets 57
Fonagy, P. 37
Fox, Jenifer 103
Fox-Eades, Jenny 57
Frederickson, Barbara 217
Freud, Sigmund 11, 67
Friedlander, B.S. 116

Gable, Shelly 202
Get Dressed activity 186
Get Moving
    Five Categories of Movement activity 148–9
    links to curriculum 27
    My Activity Dairy 151
    structure of 143–7
    Visualise Success activity 150

Get Out of Your Comfort Zone activity 159
Girlguiding UK 8
Goldstein, Sam 21, 37, 89
Greenberg, M. 39
Grogan, S. 7, 14
Grotberg, Edith H. 89, 235
group work 61
growth mindsets 57, 58

Handling Sensitive or Controversial Issues
    (PHSE Association) 226
Hanesian, H. 40
hard to reach pupils
    in learning environment 56–7
Hargreaves, E.H. 18
Harter, S. 18
Hartley-Brewer, Elizabeth 152
Hattie, J. 56
Have Fun
    A Really Fun Time activity 157
    Are You a Good Sport? activity 158
    Get Out of Your Comfort Zone activity 159
    links to curriculum 28
    structure of 152–6
    Three Sorts of Fun activity 160
Hayes, S. 7
Healthy Eating Habits: Three to Remember
    Eat a Mix of Foods Every Day activity 137
    Healthy Eating Habits Worksheet 138
    I am Full Up activity 141
    I am Hungry activity 140
    Is Eating a Pleasure or a Pastime
        for You? activity 139
    links to curriculum 26–7
    My Food Diary activity 142–3
    structure of 130–6
Healthy Eating Habits Worksheet 138
Healthy Habits Build a Positive Body Image activity 86
Healthy Habits: Looking After Ourselves activity 128
Herbert, P.C. 35
Here and Now
    background notes to 112
    Box Breathing activity 119
    links to curriculum 26
    My Mindfulness Diary 120
    structure of 113–18
Holt, K. 65
How Children Succeed (Tough) 58
How to be a Friend
    It's Good News activity 207
    It's How You Say It activity 208–9
    links to curriculum 32

How to be a Friend *cont.*
    structure of 202–5
    What Did I Learn? activity 209–10
    What Makes a Good Friend? activity 206
How to be an Amazing Talk Partner activity 88
Hughes, G. 44
Hutchinson, N. 18, 19

I am Full Up activity 141
I am Hungry activity 140
I'm, Like, So Fat! (Neumark–Sztainer) 14
Image and Appearance of the Human Body,
    The (Schilder) 11, 67
Instead of Watching TV I Could...activity 165
Introduction to the Positive Body Image programme
    Healthy Habits Build a Positive
        Body Image activity 86
    How to be an Amazing Talk Partner activity 88
    links to curriculum 24
    Our Class Rules activity 87
    structure of 81–5
Is Eating a Pleasure or a Pastime for You? activity 139
It's Good News activity 207
It's How You Say It activity 208–9

Jensen, B.B. 59
Johnson, Susan L. 130

Kater, Kathy 12, 18, 69, 70
Kazdin, A.E. 37
Keeping Children Safe in Education
    (Department for Education) 8
Knobloch-Westernick, S. 18
Kostarova-Unkovska, L. 59

learning environment
    asking questions in 55
    ground rules for 54–5
    hard to reach pupils support 56–7
    importance of 53–4
    metacognition in 58–9
    mindsets in 57, 58
    praise in 58
    relationships in 56
    vulnerable pupils support 55–6
learning objectives 45
    in Build Your Bounce Back Muscles 90
    in Get Moving 143
    in Have Fun 152
    in Healthy Eating Habits: Three to Remember 130
    in Here and Now 113

    in How to be a Friend 202
    in Introduction to the Positive Body
        Image programme 81
    in My ABC 196
    in My Hero 211
    in Pictures, Pictures Everywhere! 180
    in Strengths Spotting 103
    in Television Turnoff 161
    in The Real You 121
    in Think Twice 168
    in Thought Catching 187
    in WOOP 217
learning outcomes 45
    in Build Your Bounce Back Muscles 90
    in Get Moving 143
    in Have Fun 152
    in Healthy Eating Habits: Three to Remember 130
    in Here and Now 113
    in How to be a Friend 202–3
    in Introduction to the Positive Body
        Image programme 81
    in My ABC 196
    in My Hero 211
    in Pictures, Pictures Everywhere! 180
    in Strengths Spotting 103
    in Television Turnoff 161
    in The Real You 121
    in Think Twice 168
    in Thought Catching 187
    in WOOP 217–18
Let's Go Shopping activity 177
Lieberman, Matthew 161, 202
Linley, Alex 103
Lohrmann, D.K. 35
Look the Part: The High-Power Pose activity 102

MacConville, R.M. 19, 58
MacLean, Kerry Lee 114, 116
Masten, Anne 37, 89
Mayo, E. 175
McCabe, M.P. 65
Media Messages activity 179
metacognition
    in learning environment 58–9
Miltner, W.H.R. 57
Mindful Monkey, Happy Panda (Alderfer
    and Maclean) 114–15
mindfulness 112, 113–18
mindsets 57, 58
Mischel, Walter 21
More ABC activity 201

My ABC
    links to curriculum 31
    More ABC activity 201
    My ABC activity 200
    structure of 196–9
My ABC activity 200
My Activity Dairy 151
My Best Time activity 110
My Bounce Back Muscles activity 95–7
My Bounce Back Muscles Quiz 98, 235
My Bounce Back Muscles Record Sheet 100
My Bounce Back Shield activity 99
My Everyday Hero activity 216
My Family Tree activity 127
My Favourite Advert activity 178
My Fit Prime Time activity 167
My Food Diary activity 142–3
My Hero
    links to curriculum 33
    My Everyday Hero activity 216
    My Hero activity 215
    structure of 211–14
My Hero activity 215
My Mindfulness Diary 120

Nairn, A. 175
National Curriculum
    in Positive Body Image programme 23–34
National Institute for Health and Care Excellence 15
negative body image see body dissatisfaction
Neumark-Sztainer, Dianne 14
Novak, J. 40

Ofsted
    and parental involvement 225
    in Positive Body Image programme 24–34
Optimistic Child, The (Seligman) 38
Orbach, S. 7
Our Class Rules activity 87

parents
    and body image 231
    importance of involvement 225–6
    letter to 23
    and My Bounce Back Muscles Quiz 235
    and positive body image 230, 232, 234
    practical considerations 226–7
    resources for 236
    strengths-based approach 233
    workshop for 227–36
Parker, J.G. 202
Paxton, S. 14
personal, social, health and economic education
    in Positive Body Image programme 23–34

Peterson, Chris 76
Philips, Katherine 15
Pictures, Pictures Everywhere!
    Get Dressed activity 186
    links to curriculum 30
    structure of 180–4
    Think Real: Positive Thinking Habits activity 185
positive body image
    description of 12
    key characteristics 13
    parental training on 230, 232, 234
    staff training on 68, 72–5
Positive Body Image programme
    and active learning strategies 35
    approaches for 36–8
    assessment of 44–7
    confidentiality 50–3
    curriculum links 23–34
    description of 36
    different learning needs in 62–3
    disclosures 51–3
    evaluation of 44–7
    facilitator reflection 48–50
    learning environment for 53–9
    planning for 40
    resources for 47–8
    safeguarding 50–3
    scheduling 39–40
    settings for 8
    strategies for 59–62
    structure of 40–4
    timings for 39–40
    whole school involvement 38–9
positive psychology 86–7
    in staff training 76
praise
    in learning environment 58
programme log 47
PSHE Association 40, 44, 45, 46, 49, 50,
    51, 53, 55, 56, 59, 61, 226
Public Health England 38

Qualifications and Curriculum Authority 45

Radford, Andrew 17
random pairing 60
Real Kids Come in All Sizes (Kater) 12
Reflections on Body Image (APPG) 20, 65, 71, 72, 73
Reiher, Robert 168
relationships
    in learning environment 56
resilience building 21–2, 37
    and Build Your Bounce Back Muscles 91–2
Ricciardelli, L.A. 65

Right Now activity 47–8
    and Build Your Bounce Back Muscles 92
    and Get Moving 146
    and Have Fun 154
    and Healthy Eating Habits: Three
        to Remember 132, 134
    and How to be a Friend 204
    and Introduction to the Positive Body
        Image programme 83
    and My ABC 198
    and My Hero 213
    and Pictures, Pictures Everywhere! 183
    and Strengths Spotting 106
    and Television Turnoff 162
    and The Real You 124
    and Think Twice 171, 172
    and Thought Catching 189
    and WOOP 219
Roehlkepartain, E.C. 103
Roffey, S. 44, 56, 59
Roth, A. 37
Rumsey, Nicola 20
Ryan, R.M. 55, 89

safeguarding 50–3
Sauer, A. 57
Scales, P.C. 103
Schilder, Paul Ferdinand 11, 67
Schor, J.B. 161
Screen Time activity 166
self-esteem 11–12
    in staff training 68
Seligman, Martin 36, 37, 76, 187
sensitive issues
    and parental involvement 226
    staff training on 78
Shop Smart activity 176
Social: Why Brains are Wired to Connect (Lieberman) 202
spiritual, moral, social and cultural development
    description of 23-4
    in Positive Body Image programme 24–34
staff training
    active learning strategies 77
    approach of 65–6
    and body image 66–75
    celebrations 79
    resources for 80
    sensitive issues 78
    strengths-based approach 75–6
    support for 49
    workshop for 66–80
Stewart-Brown, S. 39
Storm in a Teacup activity 195

Story of Childhood, The: Growing Up in
    Modern Britain (Brooks) 16
Storyboard – Bounce Back: Bounce
    Forward activity 101
strategies for programme
    answering questions 61–2
    classroom talk 59
    for different learning needs 62–3
    and disability 63
    group work 61
    random pairing 60
    Talk Partners 59–60
    whole-class questions 60
Straube, T. 57
Strengths Spotting
    At My Very Best activity 112
    links to curriculum 25
    My Best Time activity 110
    Strengths Spotting activity 108–9
    structure of 103–7
Strengths Spotting activity 108–9
structure of sessions 40–4
Syvertsen, A.K. 103

Take Away activities 48
    and Build Your Bounce Back Muscles 93–4
    and Get Moving 147
    and Have Fun 155
    and Healthy Eating Habits: Three to Remember 136
    and Here and Now 117–18
    and How to be a Friend 204
    and Introduction to the Positive Body
        Image programme 84
    in My ABC 198
    and Pictures, Pictures Everywhere! 184
    and Strengths Spotting 106
    and Television Turnoff 162, 163
    and The Real You 125
    and Think Twice 172
    and Thought Catching 191
Talk Partners 59–60, 61, 62
    and Build Your Bounce Back Muscles 91, 92
    and Get Moving 145
    and Healthy Eating Habits: Three to Remember 134
    and Here and Now 114, 117
    and Introduction to the Positive Body
        Image programme 83
    and My Hero 212, 213–14
    and Pictures, Pictures Everywhere! 182
    and The Real You 123, 124
    and Think Twice 170, 171
    and Thought Catching 190
Tantleff-Dunn, S. 7

Television Turnoff
  Instead of Watching TV I Could...activity 165
  links to curriculum 28
  My Fit Prime Time activity 167
  Screen Time activity 166
  structure of 161–4
Ten Healthy Messages activity 221–2
The Real You
  All About Me activity 126
  Celebrate All the Things Your Body
    Can Do activity 129
  Healthy Habits: Looking After Ourselves activity 128
  links to curriculum 26
  My Family Tree activity 127
  structure of 121–5
Think Real: Positive Thinking Habits activity 185
Think Twice
  Children's Manifesto activity 175
  Let's Go Shopping activity 177
  links to curriculum 29
  Media Messages activity 179
  My Favourite Advert activity 178
  Shop Smart activity 176
  structure of 168–72
  What's Going On? activity 173–4
Thought Catching
  Catch That Thought activity 192
  links to curriculum 30
  Storm in a Teacup activity 195
  structure of 187–91
  Tricky Situations activity 193–4
Three Sorts of Fun activity 160
Thuen, E. 55

Tiggemann, M. 14, 18
Tobias, S.E. 116
Tough, P. 58
Tricky Situations activity 193–4
Turner, Sally 112
Tylka, T.L. 13

Visualise Success activity 150
vulnerable pupils
  support for 55–6

Walker, D.L. 202
Wallace, S.A. 37
Weichselbaum, E. 38
Weisz, J.R. 37
Wells, J. 39
Wertheim, E. 14
What Did I Learn? activity 209–10
What's Going On? activity 173–4
What Makes a Good Friend? activity 206
whole-class discussions 60
  and Strengths Spotting 105
Wilson, Timothy 49
WOOP
  certificate for 219–20, 224
  links to curriculum 34
  structure of 217–20
  Ten Healthy Messages activity 221–2
  WOOP activity 223
WOOP activity 223
Working Together to Safeguard Children
  (Department for Education) 8

Dr Ruth MacConville is an educational consultant, and formerly worked as Head of the Special Educational Needs Service in Ealing, London. She is the author of several books on promoting happiness, resilience and well-being in young people. She lives in London, UK.